Carving
Realistic Birds

Carving
Realistic Birds

David Tippey

GUILD OF MASTER CRAFTSMAN PUBLICATIONS LTD

First published 1996 by
Guild of Master Craftsman Publications Ltd,
166 High Street, Lewes,
East Sussex BN7 1XU

© David Tippey 1996

ISBN 1 86108 010 7

Photography © David Tippey, except photographs on
pages 84, 108 and 126, and all,
photographs in Chapter 14, courtesy of
Windrush Photographic Agency

Carving Designs © David Tippey

Line drawings by John Yates, except
Figs 5.9, 5.19, and 5.22 by David Tippey

Designed by Ian Hunt Design

Typeface: Perpetua

Origination by Master Image Ltd, Singapore
Printed by the University Press, Cambridge

CONTENTS

Measurements and References

MEASUREMENTS

Although care has been taken to ensure that imperial measurements are true and accurate, they are only conversions from metric. Instances will be found where a metric measurement has fractionally varying imperial equivalents (or vice versa), usually within ½in either way. This is because, in each particular case, the closest imperial equivalent has been given, rounding up or down to the nearest ½in.

PAINTS AND PAINT MIXES

All paints used in this book are Jo Sonja Acrylic Gouache unless otherwise stated.

All paint mixes are a guide only—colour variations are wide. The mix forms a good starting point, but isn't the only way of achieving that colour. Additional reference material is essential as these basic painting instructions cannot convey all the subtleties of feather colour.

SUPPLIERS

To locate stockists and suppliers of materials referred to in this book, please consult your local telephone directory or related magazines. For suppliers in the UK, consult any copy of *Woodcarving* or *Woodworker* magazine. For suppliers in the USA and Canada, consult any copy of *Wildfowl Carving and Collecting* or the March/April edition of *Chip Chats*, which contains an annual review of suppliers.

ACKNOWLEDGEMENTS

I would like to thank the many people, including family, friends, customers and fellow carvers, who have given their help, support and encouragement to my carving and writing.

More specifically I would like to thank my wife Angela for her unstinting support since my interest in bird carving was first awakened.

INTRODUCTION

Bird carving as it is seen today springs from the efforts of American carvers to preserve the techniques of the traditional decoy carvings of the late nineteenth and early twentieth centuries, whilst continuing the development of the genre into a sophisticated medium beyond simply emulating the work of past carvers.

It is generally accepted that the hunting decoy was developed by the European settlers from hunting methods employed by the native Americans. In 1924, reed canvasback decoys, estimated to be almost 2,000 years old, were found in a Nevada cave. The settlers took to decoys like a 'duck to water' and the combination of decoy and gun was devastating! At the end of the nineteenth century, thousands of decoys were deployed to lure ducks and geese migrating along the traditional flyways, to the guns of the market hunters below. It was soon realized that shooting on this scale was unsustainable, and by the early twentieth century market gunning had been banned and decoys were only needed for the small rigs used by individual hunters.

This brought about the demise of most of the factory-produced decoys, which had their heyday in the mid to late nineteenth century, leaving individual makers, and the hunters themselves, to supply the diminished market. The great number of individual carvers involved meant that there was a huge diversity in style, construction and painting, and this led to the better preserved examples becoming very collectable as objects of folk art.

Hunting decoys continued to be carved and used for their original purpose, but the upsurge in interest in the decoy as an art object, particularly after WWII, brought about refreshed interest in decoy carving and the more detailed decoys that came to be known as 'decoratives'. Competitions for decoy carvings were held, often in association with shooting clubs, and these competitions, originally for purely

functional hunting decoys, started to attract more carvings intended to be ornamental rather than functional. The end of the 1960s saw the birth of realistic bird carvings as we know them today, when someone took an electric soldering iron to their bird and burnt on feather markings for the first time.

Since then new tools and techniques have constantly been added to the repertoire of the carver, so that now a bird carving by a top class carver can hardly be

Ruddy turnstone shorebird decoy, traditional style.

Golden eagle head and peregrine falcon (4in (102mm) miniature).

distinguished from the real thing. The subject range has grown too; no longer confined to luring other birds to the gun, any species which catches the imagination can be carved, from humble sparrows to majestic eagles.

ART OR CRAFT?

Wildlife artists have always been the Cinderellas of the art world – just on the fringe of acceptability – probably because much of the work produced, like the work of the botanical artist, has more in common

Stylized carvings are less time-consuming than realistic birds.

with illustration than what would usually be accepted as 'true art'. The trend in much modern wildlife art, especially American, for realism rather than stylization leaves artists branded as technicians and illustrators by the mainstream art world.

It may be said that artists generally produce works which are truly unique, even if conceived as part of an ongoing series, or developing a theme, whilst craftworkers tend to develop designs which are then replicated, with only minor variations inherent in the individual crafting of the pieces, though some, of course, produce a blend of the two, especially when trying to become established in a very difficult market.

As the techniques of realistic bird carving improved, subjects tended to be presented in wildlife dioramas, much like taxidermy, fuelling the argument that the works were not art but craft. Now that the ultimate goal of total realism in bird carving has virtually been achieved, artists are putting more thought into the presentation and design of carvings. Carvings are starting to be presented in a more sculptural context, and a trend towards stylization used in combination with realistic elements is starting – surely a sign that bird carving is growing into a real 'artform' and may even, one day, become accepted in mainstream art circles.

WHY AND WHAT TO CARVE

Such debates are not what draw people to carving birds though, but a fascination with the techniques, the new possibilities they provide and, usually, a fondness for, and interest in, living birds.

Almost all the practical bird carving books come from North America – hardly surprising as this is where the carving style was developed – and the vast majority of these are concerned with the traditional decoy species of waterfowl. If ducks attract you and are what you want to carve, then this situation is reasonably satisfactory, as many of the American species are also European natives or at least are seen in waterfowl collections here. The few

American books that do cover small birds contain mainly species which are unknown in Europe – very few of our common woodland and garden birds are represented on both sides of the Atlantic. One or two of these small North American birds can be disguised as their European counterparts as they are similar, but there are variations in size and markings. This book is an attempt to redress the balance for the European bird carver. I decided that there must be a place on any carver's bookshelf for a book with a more European flavour, and this is the result.

Turning the tables, European species can be disguised as their American counterparts and there are some species that are also found in North America.

With that, I hope this book will also appeal to carvers on the other side of the Atlantic who may be looking for something different to carve, perhaps as a reminder of the countries that they or their ancestors emigrated from. I recently had a special request from North America, from a lady who told me that European robins still conjured up thoughts of winter and Christmas for her; even though she had lived in Canada for many years, the American robin just wasn't the same!

Stylized birds can highlight the tactile properties of carvings.

TOOLS AND TECHNIQUES

People are generally fascinated by realistic bird carvings, finding it difficult to believe that they are not covered with real feathers. Many carvers feel the urge to try it themselves on seeing a high quality, realistic bird carving for the first time: this book is intended to be a thorough introduction to the special tools, techniques and skills required to enable them to do just that. Although it is primarily intended to serve as a reference source for more experienced carvers attempting this style of work for the first time, sufficient information is included for the confident novice.

Left: Pied Flycatcher (*Ficedula hypoleuca*).

CHAPTER 1

SAFETY

Looking after your health and safety is most important. All sorts of rules and regulations exist to protect you at work, but legislation barely touches the hobbyist – it is only prudent to carry out your own health and safety audit and assessment of the way you work. These precautions are basically just good workshop practice and common sense, but hopefully they will prompt you to address any areas you may have overlooked. I already had a problem with house dust and tobacco smoke, so it was no surprise to find I was also affected by wood dust. Taking sensible precautions before problems arise will help prevent you ending up with breathing disorders; don't wait for the problems to show up, act first!

WORKING WITH POWER TOOLS

When using power carving equipment, you should observe the standard workshop precautions as regards securing loose clothing and long hair, and it is also very wise to follow these additional safety precautions:

ALWAYS WEAR SUITABLE, APPROVED EYE PROTECTION Abrasive stones, brushes, solid carbide burrs, and sanders are all prone to shedding bits through wear and tear or breakage. Your eyes are particularly vulnerable when working on small detailed work because of the proximity of the work to your face. Face shields, especially large ones, may not give adequate protection when working close to your project as they may allow debris to come up behind the visor and into your eyes.

WEAR A MASK OR RESPIRATOR Wood dust is proven to be hazardous to your respiratory system and precautions should

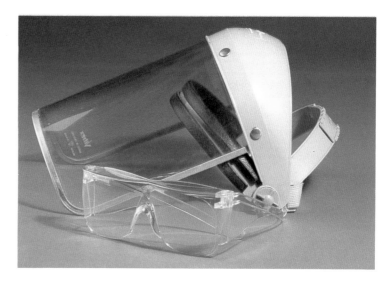

be taken, even when working for a very short time. Make sure that the mask or respirator you use is of a suitable specification for working with fine wood dust. Disposable masks are quite good unless you wear glasses or have a beard, in which case they mist up your glasses and don't seal to your face! A powered respirator, preferably the type with a flip-up visor (for convenience when drinking your coffee), is a better bet for regular use.

USE A DUST EXTRACTOR Dust extraction is not a luxury but an absolute necessity if you power carve often. It is an adjunct and not an alternative to the use of personal respiratory protection. Keep the dust extraction points as near as possible to your work so that it catches the smaller, lighter particles efficiently. The very fine dust created by small burrs or by sanding will stay suspended in the air for you to breathe in long after you have finished work and removed your mask. Make sure that you are using a dust extractor and not a chip extractor which is intended for larger particles and shavings from machines such as saws and planers, and will allow many of the smaller, harmful dust particles through.

Fig 1.1 Eye protection is essential when working with power tools.

KEEP THE WORKSHOP AREA CLEAN The fine dust will build up to a thick layer over everything and will be constantly disturbed and breathed in when you are in the workshop. Keeping your work area dust free will also give you a better environment for spreading out your research materials to assist you while you carve. Dust is also a fire and explosion hazard, so a little weekly housekeeping with the vacuum cleaner could save more than your health, as well as giving you a more pleasant working environment.

WEAR SAFETY CLOTHING Every motorcyclist knows that leathers are the best protection against abrasions when you come off your bike; the same is true for carving burrs. They will rip through a shirt and viciously attack you given half a chance, and they make a tremendous job of chewing up pullovers, not to mention the potential damage to the power carver itself. Breakage of the inner shaft is most probable, and damage to the outer shaft is possible as well, if you wind your sweater round the burr. A closely-woven cotton work smock, apron or overall will afford some protection, as it gives less for the burr to grab at, but a leather apron offers by far the best protection. For the same reason, beginners may like to wear a leather glove on their work-holding hand. Leather aprons also give good protection to the thighs from knife cuts when carvings are held on your lap.

SWITCHES AND CABLES Keep the foot control in a safe position where you will not accidentally step on it. Industrial foot switches are usually protected by an arched cover that you put your foot into – an easy DIY modification. Keep the cables away from the hand piece, to prevent damage by cutters, and away from your feet, and finally, try to remember to switch off the machine at the mains when it is not in use.

SKIN PROTECTION Many people find that the fine dust produced when sanding causes irritation to the skin, especially between the fingers. Eventually your skin may become

Fig 1.2 Dust protection can range from a simple paper mask to a full-face, powered respirator.

Fig 1.3 Leather apron, glove and thumb guard: leather is the best protection against attacks by power carving tools.

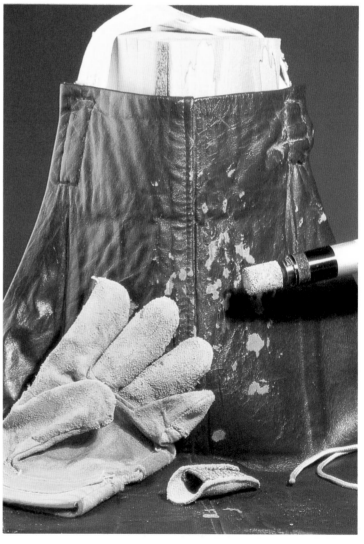

sensitized to materials you regularly work with and a minor irritation can become a more serious case of dermatitis. The use of suitable barrier creams can help prevent conditions developing.

USING A PYROGRAPHY PEN

Although, in essence, the pyrograph is a very simple device, it does present potential hazards to health and home, and some precautions are necessary.

Good ventilation is essential, as the smoke from burning is an irritant and could possibly be harmful in the long term; I use a small fan which I sit on the workbench, or run the dust extractor to draw the smoke away from my face. Take great care when burning any areas with glue or filler on them, as the heat is likely to break these down and give off toxic fumes.

The burning pen should not just be laid on the bench, as the tip is hot enough to burn through the insulation on the electric cables or, on its hottest settings, even ignite flammable material. Keep the bench clear of rubbish and flammable items and put the pen back into its clip when you are not using it, safely away from the mains lead.

HANDLING DEAD BIRDS

When handling taxidermy specimens or dead birds, do not smoke or eat, and make sure you wash your hands thoroughly; this is good hygiene with a modern taxidermy mount, but many older specimens were preserved using dangerous chemicals like arsenic, so hygiene becomes much more important. Dead birds are best treated by carefully wrapping them, sealing in a plastic bag, and then freezing them: this will kill off parasites and some disease organisms. They should be handled wearing surgical gloves, and if taxidermy is not intended, disposed of as soon as possible after notes, sketches and samples have been collected.

WORKING WITH GLUES, SOLVENTS AND FILLERS

Read the instructions that come with glues, solvents and fillers: I know these are the words that we normally resort to when all else fails and not before, but they do inform us of any specific hazards and precautions necessary when handling the product.

Make sure that you have an adequately ventilated work area when handling any product which contains solvents or gives off fumes, however innocuous these products may seem.

Try to keep glues, fillers and solvents off your skin; if used regularly your skin may become sensitized to the chemicals, causing dermatitis. The use of suitable barrier creams can help prevent problems, and disposable gloves should be used for handling solvents and glues. Latex or vinyl surgical-style gloves are much better than the cheap, badly-fitting polythene kind, and are readily available at chemists.

When using superglues, keep them away from inquisitive children, and have a bottle of skin de-bonder handy so that you can release yourself from your carving when the glue runs further than you expected!

CHAPTER 2

TOOLS

Creating the basic form of the bird can be completed using whatever tools you feel most comfortable with, or perhaps just happen to own. Depending on the scale and subject anything to hand, including penknives, saws, rasps, files, gouges, spokeshaves, drawknives, or even an axe, could be used to manually shape the initial form, and if you are into power tools you can add chainsaws, angle grinders, sanders, power files and flexi-shaft carving machines! However, once the basic form is achieved, some more specialized equipment is necessary to create the details and realistic feather texturing that this type of carving requires, and it is these tools which I will cover here, in detail.

POWER CARVING TOOLS

Power tools are essential to achieve the effects needed for realistic bird carving. Flexible shaft power carving machines are invaluable both as general carving tools and as a texturing machine, but if you cannot afford one, then a mini drill/grinder, of the type used by model makers, can be pressed into service for texturing. Although much of the basic carving and shaping can be done with general carving tools, texturing and fine detailing requires the use of a power tool, and once you have used a good grinder to carve and texture, you will appreciate the control and delicacy of touch that it gives.

Using a proper flexible shaft power carving machine and appropriate cutters can be likened to the freedom experienced in

Fig 2.1 A wide range of hand tools are suitable for initial carving and shaping, but for detailing, some specialist tools are required.

Fig 2.2 A pyrograph is essential for burning feather barbs, and a small grinder is necessary for texturing.

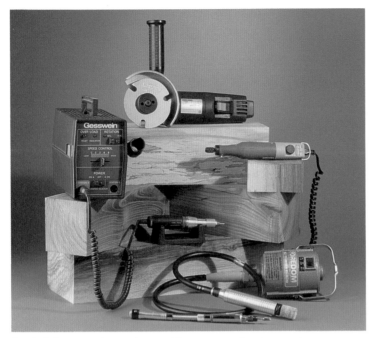

Fig 2.3 Power tools can be used for carving, shaping, and some specialist texturing techniques.

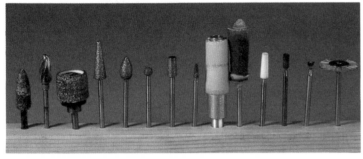

Fig 2.4 An initial set of tools for use in a flexi-shaft carving machine.

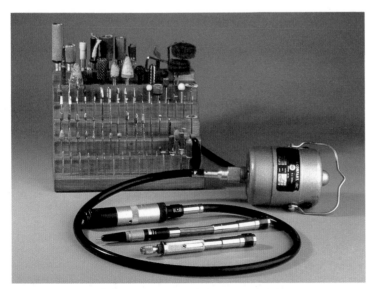

Fig 2.5 Eventually, you will probably acquire a kit of tools like this: tool buying can be addictive.

sketching, or clay modelling: the wood yields easily, uniformly and quickly, letting you concentrate on essential line and form, enabling beginners and more experienced carvers alike, to concentrate on the subject rather than the techniques of tool usage. Learning to control a power carver is a much quicker experience than mastering the use of edge tools, and they open up a whole new dimension to woodcarving! The larger, more powerful machines are capable of heavy roughing out as well. They free your creativity, but more importantly, enable you to perform the delicate carving tasks and texturing required in realistic bird carving; operations which are not possible with conventional tools.

Despite many people's hopes, a power drill with a flexible shaft is no substitute for the proper machine. The shafts are too stiff to be properly controlled, and drill motor speeds are too slow for anything but sanding. However, they can be useful if you are using large sanding drums on big projects, because it is difficult to keep the speed low enough with the foot control of a proper power carver.

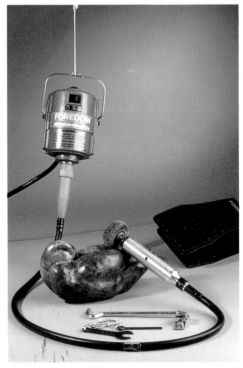

Fig 2.6 Larger machines will cope with the demands of heavy carving and sanding.

MAINTENANCE

Small, light duty flexible shaft machines are cheaper and will happily cope with light carving and texturing, though they may give some trouble if they are asked to perform heavy work, which they weren't designed for. One of the smaller, entry level machines will probably last years when used for detailing and texturing in timbers like jelutong, but may fail in weeks if used for heavy roughing out work. If your budget only runs to one of the smaller machines or a model makers' mini drill/grinder, then look after it by using sharp cutters, letting them cut at their own speed, and not using excessive pressure. You will get better results and a longer machine life for your trouble. Professional carvers often use very high speed, miniature, electric or air-powered die grinders (specialist miniature grinders); these are too expensive to be entertained by most amateur carvers, and I consider that they only offer marginal advantage over a good flexible shaft carving machine.

CUTTERS

Cutters are very important to the proper working of these machines and good ones are not cheap, so make sure you budget for a few good quality cutters to start off with. Traditional toothed cutters, like milling cutters or router bits, are not very suitable for general use as their cutting action is affected by the variations in the timber, caused by the grain. Abrasive burrs are much more suitable and less likely to tear the timber. Carbon, and even high speed steel cutters quickly become blunt, so the best option for general carving and shaping is a tungsten carbide grinding cutter. Although these are more expensive initially, their working life is very long and so, as is the case with most tools, they are the best buy in the end. Diamond and ruby burrs are suitable for finer detail carving, and abrasive grindstones for very fine carving and texturing. People tend to collect cutters like stamps, often thinking that you need a

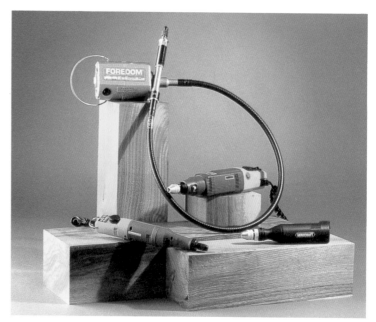

Fig 2.7 Light duty, flexi-shaft carvers and mini drills are suitable for light carving and texturing only.

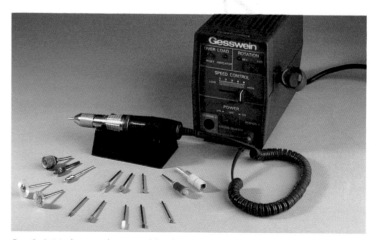

Fig 2.8 High speed, reversible die grinders are used by many serious bird carvers for texturing.

Fig 2.9 Toothed carbide cutters have a tendency to rip out grain.

Fig 2.10 Three small tools used for initial shaping. Left: a structured carbide burr. Centre: a ¾in (19mm) drum sander. Right: a toothed carbide dental cutter.

Fig 2.11 Tungsten carbide burrs are usually used for initial shaping.

particular cutter to do a particular job because a 'well-known carver' always uses that one. In most cases there is not just a single cutter that is suitable for a particular job; although a particular cutter may feature in the following carvings, make use of the ones you own first before dashing out to buy any more. It is the man behind the tool that is the most important factor, not the particular tool!

TUNGSTEN CARBIDE CUTTERS

Carbide cutters with conventional formed and ground teeth will cut cleanly, but they are still subject to the vagaries of grain direction and to knots. Carbide, rasp-style cutters leave a rougher finish, but their cutting action is largely unaffected by the

timber they are working on. Tungsten carbide cutters do, of course, cost much more, but like carbide sawblades and router cutters they last much longer – my oldest sintered carbide cutter is six years old and still going strong! Good, sharp cutters mean that less pressure need be applied, causing less strain on the machine and leaving the operator with more control over the tool, so keep them clean! Carbide cutters are available either with structured, needle-like teeth or with the tungsten carbide particles bonded randomly to the surface. Both types can be cleaned by soaking them in paint stripper or oven cleaner, and then rinsing them off under a tap and brushing with a brass wire brush. Alternatively, they can be burnt clean with a small blowtorch flame. The finish from these cutters varies from a coarse, rasped surface to a medium, sandpapered one; beware though, the scratches left by the teeth of coarse-structured carbide cutters can be very deep, and work should be started with a finer grade at an earlier stage than might be anticipated!

DIAMOND AND RUBY ABRASIVE BURRS

Detailing work and finer carving and shaping are best performed with cutters made by plating abrasive synthetic ruby or diamond particles onto a mandrel. They are kept clean by running them against the rubber cleaning blocks that are sold for use with belt sanders. If they do become really clogged, use the paint stripper treatment.

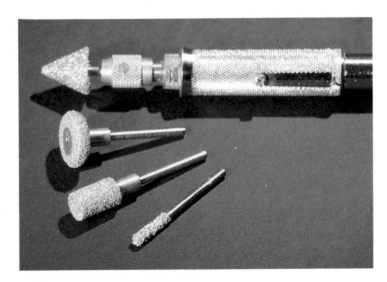

Fig 2.12 Ruby carvers are usually used for refining detail carving.

Fig 2.13 Diamond cutters are generally finer than ruby carvers, and are available in much smaller shapes for very fine work.

Diamond burrs can be re-dressed to expose fresh diamond cutting facets by running them against specially produced, fine abrasive stones, but do so with care or you may only be left with the mandrel! Although both diamond and ruby carvers are available in different grades, the ruby carvers tend to be coarser than the diamond burrs, but both leave a medium to fine sanded finish.

SMALL ABRASIVE GRINDSTONES

Small aluminium oxide and similar abrasive stones are available in a wide variety of shapes and grades. The coarser ones, usually coloured, can be used for carving work similarly to diamond and ruby carvers, but they clog up faster. The very fine white stones are particularly good for texturing and smoothing wood to a polished finish. When clogged, they can have a fresh surface revealed by running them against a coarser stone, a diamond file or an old diamond burr. They can also be formed into your own special shapes in the same way. They should never be heated or treated with paint stripper to unclog them, as it will affect the bonding to the shaft, making them potentially dangerous.

SANDERS

Small sanders for use in power carving machines come in various guises – some are more use than others. The small, rigid, sleeve sanding drums are not very good at smoothing surfaces as they dig in and bounce, but they do perform well at roughing out and carving, when fitted with a coarse sleeve.

Fig 2.15 Various sanding attachments can be used with a flexi-shaft to speed up sanding, but most are only useful on larger surfaces, and they must be run slowly enough.

Fig 2.16 Small sanders for small carvings. Left: a ⅜in (10mm) soft sander covered with neoprene foam, takes ordinary sanding cloth. Right: a split sanding mandrel, wound with abrasive tape.

Fig 2.14 Small abrasive stones, available in various shapes, sizes and grits, are used for fine detail carving and texturing.

The latest type of soft sander is the miniature pneumatic sanding drum, where you inflate a rubber bulb to hold the sanding sleeve in place. You can vary the hardness of the drum by the amount of air used to inflate it, but again, you have to buy ready-made sleeves.

BRUSHES

Small brushes are used to remove dust, debris and charred wood from the texturing of carvings. Old toothbrushes are very useful for this, but hard and soft bristle, miniature rotary brushes are often used before and after sealing a carving.

PYROGRAPHS

The other specialized piece of equipment used by carvers of realistic birds is the pyrograph. The pyrographs used for bird carving are highly specialized, and the majority of pyrographs on the UK market

Fig 2.17 The pneumatic sander, the latest soft sander, will conform to surfaces, but its size prevents it being used for very small birds.

Fig 2.18 Brushes used to clean carving and burning debris from texturing. Left: soft nylon bristles. Right: stiffer bristles which will remove wood fibres hardened by sealer.

Cartridge sanding rolls screw onto a tapered pigtail-type mandrel, but they also bounce and the abrasive rapidly wears away, exposing the metal mandrel. A split mandrel around which you wind abrasive, securing it with a piece of adhesive tape, works as well, if not better, and is often used for initial sanding of feather groups.

Soft sanders are cushioned with foam and out-perform all the previous types — they have little tendency to bounce and dig in, and so give good smooth surfaces. They also have the advantage of taking cut pieces of abrasive material rather than expensive ready-made sleeves, and are made in a variety of sizes.

Fig 2.19 Pyrographs can be used to clean up awkward corners and produce fine undercuts on feathers.

are not really suitable. The three essential features needed in a pyrograph for bird carving are:

1 variable temperature;

2 fine knife-like points; and

3 controllability.

Fixed temperature types which are made like soldering irons really fail on all three counts:

1 they have no real temperature control unless connected to an external power controller;

2 they have clumsy, large soldering iron points; and

3 their handle is too far from the tip to give any real control.

Ordinary, heated wire handpieces are great for drawing and writing on wood, but are not suitable for the type of markings that are required for bird carving. The machines specifically designed for the job have handpieces with the tips formed from heavy resistance wire, forged and ground into various shapes. Because the tip is directly heated by a variable electric current passing through it, the fingertips can be held very close to the tip without them burning, giving very good control over its movement. The proper tool is not simply used for marking feathers, but is used as a carving tool for cleaning awkward areas, undercutting feathers, forming feather splits, smoothing and burnishing areas, as well as many other jobs.

Many shapes of tip are available, but initially I would recommend buying the general purpose, oblique, pointed knife blade (Detailmaster 1C) and the small, tight, round knife tip (Detailmaster 2B) for general work. These two will probably cover 95% of situations, and you can buy additional ones when they become really necessary.

If finances will not allow the purchase of one of the better units, purchase one of the shorter soldering iron types with a sharp knife tip, and control the temperature with a light-dimmer switch if no proper temperature control is fitted.

Fig 2.20 A pyrograph of the heated knife variety, specially made for feather burning.

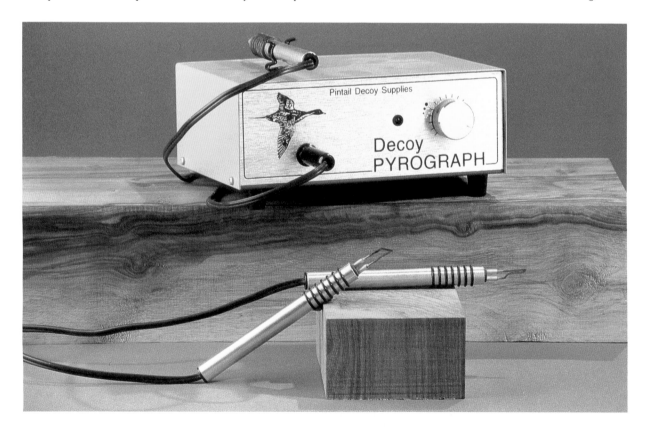

MAGNIFIERS

When burning fine, close feather lines and generally working on tight detail, some form of magnification is a real advantage. Unfortunately, my eyesight and age combine to have me frequently juggling three pairs of spectacles; normal, reading and close-up. Additionally, my workshop reading pair have flip-up binocular magnifiers fitted to them, and I also have at my disposal an illuminated stand magnifier, a headband magnifier and various jewellers' eye glasses; I have become an optical hypochondriac as my sight worsens. If you have very good eyesight, a pair of cheap, non-prescription reading glasses may be a useful aid for close-up work, but the best piece of equipment I have used, and highly recommended by other carvers, is the Optivisor binocular headband magnifier. This is rather better constructed than some of its cheaper rivals, may be worn with spectacles, is very good optically, and is far easier to use than illuminated stand magnifiers, which get in the way and cause damage to carvings. The only drawback is that it cannot be worn with a full face respirator, hence my close-up prescription glasses.

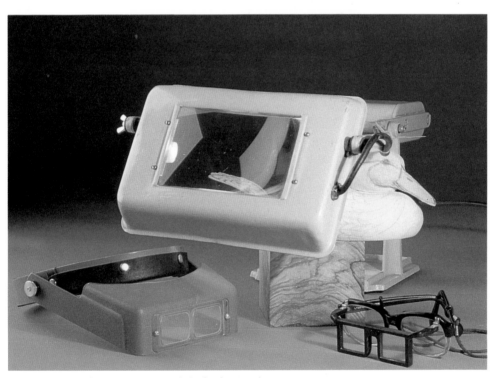

Fig 2.21 Magnification is a great help for fine work.

CHAPTER 3
MATERIALS

SUITABLE TIMBERS

The most important characteristic of timber suitable for realistic carving and texturing is the possession of a homogeneous, fine, close-grain structure. Any difference in the hardness of growth rings, as found particularly in the softwoods, will be reproduced as variations in the depth of the texturing. The relative importance of the weight and strength of the timber used varies with the demands of the design. For maximum strength in thin, vulnerable areas, it is important to try and arrange for the grain to run straight through them. This is not always possible if you want to carve the bird from one piece, so choosing a tougher timber like lime or tupelo, and arranging the grain to run correctly through the most delicate area, would be the best solution.

I have listed several timbers below that are regularly used by carvers of realistic carvings, but there are undoubtedly other suitable timbers available around the world, so if these are not available to you it would be worth experimenting.

BASSWOOD

(Tilia glabra; Tilia americana; Tilia nigra; Tilia latifolia; Tilia canadensis; Tilia heteraphylla)

This timber is also called American whitewood, lime or linden. It is the American equivalent of the European lime.

ORIGIN USA and Canada
SPECIFIC GRAVITY 0.45–0.41; 26lbs/ft³ (334kg/dm³)
COLOUR Varies from a yellowish or grayish white to pale brown, or creamy white to pale pinkish brown.
QUALITIES Fairly light, soft, not particularly strong or durable. The even, fine-textured grain is easy to work, with both hand and power tools, and it shrinks and warps freely without cracking.

AVAILABILITY Readily available in both the UK and the USA, although the material that I have bought in the UK has been quite brownish in colour, with a very marked tendency to fuzzing when texturing.

JELUTONG

(Dyera costulata and species)

A type of rubber tree, this is the most commonly used timber for realistic bird carving in the UK. Its major drawback is that it is weak and friable in thin sections, necessitating the use of inserts of other timbers for vulnerable areas.

ORIGIN Malaysia and Indonesia
SPECIFIC GRAVITY 0.48–0.46; 29lbs/ft³ (372.5kg/dm³)
COLOUR White or pale straw.
QUALITIES Light, very soft, almost like Balsa, weak and brittle. The timber is stable, with fine grain, and very easily worked. It may contain latex ducts.
AVAILABILITY Stocked fairly widely in the UK, and readily available in the USA, but its sustainability is questioned by some, as it comes from one particular area of Asia, and very high quality material is becoming more

Fig 3.1 Beautiful English hardwoods, unfortunately not suitable for realistic carvings, make wonderful bases and plinths.

expensive and difficult to obtain. I look out for the harder, heavier, white timber which I find works better than the slightly darker in colour, but lighter and softer pieces which can be very like balsa.

LIME

(Tilia vulgaris; Tilia cordata; Tilia parvifolia; Tilia platyphylla)

Native European lime, sometimes called linden. This is a favourite timber amongst European carvers.

ORIGIN Europe
SPECIFIC GRAVITY 0.52–0.54; 34lbs/ft³ (437kg/dm³)
COLOUR Pale yellowish white to brown, sometimes with a reddish tinge.
QUALITIES Relatively light and soft. The timber is stable, and the fine, close grain carves and textures well.
AVAILABILITY Cheap and easy to obtain in the UK, available from specialist outlets, but not generally available in the USA.

TUPELO GUM

(Nyssa aquatica and other *Nyssa* species including black; swamp black; and sour tupelo gums)*

Also called Nyssa poplar, bay poplar or American whitewood. It can be carved thin enough for light to pass through and still be incredibly strong. It is now my favourite timber for texturing.

ORIGIN USA
SPECIFIC GRAVITY 0.5; 31.25lbs/ft³ (401.5kg/dm³)
COLOUR Gray to light brown or ivory coloured.
QUALITIES Light, soft, stiff and strong. Its interlocking grain makes it tough and difficult to split, but with its fine, uniform texture it is easy to work. Difficult to season without warping.
AVAILABILITY Difficult to obtain in the UK and what material is available is harder, much heavier, and not as good to work as the timber I have bought from the USA, where it is readily available. However, even though the quality of the UK supplies is not so good, I think it out performs the other timbers available.

ADHESIVES

I use three types of adhesive when working on bird carvings; a general wood glue, an epoxy adhesive, and a cyanoacrylate super-glue. Glues come in many types and makes; some are general purpose types and some are specifically designed to join timber.

Fig 3.2 Top left: lime. Bottom left: tupelo. Right: jelutong. Note the latex ducts running through the small piece of jelutong: these usually end up where you don't want them.

Most of the ones likely to be of use in bird carving, and readily available for the home workshop, fall into the following six categories.

ANIMAL GLUES

Both hot and cold animal glues were the traditional means of joining timber. They are not waterproof, and have now been superseded except in some specialist applications such as restoration, where the ability to take work apart again is desirable.

Fig 3.3 The glue gun is very useful for temporary fixing and creating habitat, but not much use for general assembly work.

PVA ADHESIVES (POLYVINYL ACETATES)

These are now one of the most common types of wood glue, and are available in indoor and outdoor (water resistant) grades, some with good gap filling properties. They are white and creamy and come ready for use; when dry they are translucent. They cure by a combination of absorption and evaporation, and joints require clamping for several hours until full strength is achieved.

UREA FORMALDEHYDE ADHESIVE

The most commonly found version comes as a self-catalysing powder which is mixed with water just before use. Once mixed it has a very short life, so it needs preparing as it is required. Other types may have a separate liquid hardener which is applied to one side of the joint, so the powdered glue component can be mixed and stored for a day or so. The curing is a chemical reaction which starts when water is added to the all-in-one mix, or when the two surfaces are brought together in the case of the two-part glues. Curing times are similar to PVA adhesives, so clamping is necessary. Accelerators are available to speed up the

Fig 3.4 A selection of adhesives: the brown beads are pearl animal glue.

curing time of some types to only five minutes or so. They are very strong and water-resistant, and often used in boatbuilding.

EPOXY ADHESIVES

These consist of a two-part mix of glue and hardener which can be used to stick wood, but are generally too expensive to use for large jobs. They are readily available in small quantities, and usually come in normal and fast setting varieties. I find the fast setting varieties leave a more flexible glue line.

SUPERGLUES

Superglues come in many varieties, some for very specific applications. The general purpose varieties which will glue wood are available in thickened, gap filling, or thin and waterlike varieties. Accelerators and debonding agents are available to use with these glues.

HOT MELT ADHESIVES

Hot melt adhesives are useful for tacking and temporarily holding things in place, and sometimes in the construction of habitat, but the glue line is too thick and the working time too short to make them of much general use.

I have tried many glues for fixing heads and laminating carving blocks, with varying degrees of success. One of the problems with many glues is that the glue line reappears over a period of time, becoming visible through the paint. This is particularly noticeable with the white PVA wood-working adhesives and the rapid set epoxy glues, neither of which set rock hard. Many American carvers advocate the use of fast setting epoxy resin glues, but then they usually grind out the glue line and fill it with wood filler before texturing. If possible, I prefer not to use any filler here, and try instead to get as thin a glue line as I can, and hide the joint in the texturing.

I now use Borden, Cascamite TA200 glue – a urea formaldehyde pre-catalysed variety. This suits most of my wood gluing needs, from laminating blocks for full size

swans, to gluing on heads. It gives an extremely strong bond – usually stronger than the timber – and sets very hard, without any tendency for the glue line to creep at a later date. The normal formulation takes several hours to set, but two high speed hardeners are available to accelerate the curing time to 5 or 20 minutes with no noticeable loss in bonding strength. The 5 minute hardener makes this as quick to use as the epoxy adhesives, and it is considerably cheaper.

Gluing up bird carvings and laminating blocks often requires considerable ingenuity, and the making of specially shaped clamping blocks. For many operations I use large elastic bands, cut from various sizes of car and wagon tyre inner tubes, to apply pressure. Dowels or small veneer pins, just protruding above one of the glue faces, prevent the two pieces sliding over each other as the bands are put on. The more bands used, the more pressure is applied, and the technique often works where ordinary clamps fail.

My use of epoxy adhesive is now almost solely for gluing legs into bodies and bases, and I use both fast and slow curing varieties. It is quite stringy in use, and it is a good idea to keep a plastic bottle containing methylated spirits on the bench for removing excess epoxy from your fingers, work and clothes.

Thin, water-like superglue can be soaked into thin, vulnerable tips of bills and feathers to toughen them after texturing and burning. This must be done after burning as the fumes given off from the hot pen on the glue are toxic. I have never had particularly good success using superglues as permanent adhesives, although I find them useful for temporary assembly. If they don't cure quickly enough for you, buy some accelerator, but while you are at it buy some debonder as well, so that you can separate your fingers! Superglues can be used when making habitat to build up thin branches and the like. If you coat wire with superglue and sprinkle it with baking powder it instantly sets like concrete; keep the debonder handy!

WOOD FILLERS

Wood fillers tend to come in one of the two following types:

PLASTIC WOODS

These contain cellulose fibres as the filler, mixed in a water- or solvent-based 'glue'. The latest types are water-based, which ruin the texturing by raising the grain! The original varieties, which mainly used acetone as a solvent, can be distinguished by the flammable warning sign on their packaging. I try to avoid using them as a general filler wherever possible, but they can be used for a little judicious rebuilding of minor mistakes: with the acetone solvent (which is available from chemists) and a brush, the filler can be shaped or smoothed out to a feather edge. Plastic wood can also be used as a simple way to form eye rings. (*See* Eye rings in Chapter 9, on page 66.)

Some makes are smoother and less granular than others, and so are easier to use; I find the Cuprinol brand is particularly good. Once dry, the plastic wood can be carved, textured, or burnt on a low pyrograph setting, and can even be removed months later with the application of more acetone.

RESIN WOOD FILLERS

These are a two-part formulation of filler and hardener, similar to car body filler. I have not found these to be of much use on carvings. They set quickly and once set can be carved, but they cannot be burnt with the pyrograph to texture them, and they tend to clog rotary cutters. However, they are useful for making earth as part of a habitat; textured by stippling and pushed around with an old brush as they are setting, the effect is quite realistic. They can also be used to make convincing soft mud.

EPOXY PUTTIES

Based on an observation of their working properties when mixed, I have detected that epoxy putty is available in at least two different types (this is probably a vast over simplification, and I will now be harried by the epoxy putty experts!). Epoxy putties are usually supplied as two different coloured sticks or as a two-coloured ribbon, and the two sticks or strips are mixed in equal quantities until they have a uniform colour.

Type one (the two sticks) can be smoothed by using water and a brush, but it is crumbly and not very ductile so it cannot be stretched out into a thin ribbon. I use this type for positioning eyes, and the brand I use, Milliput, is widely available in hobby and model shops.

Type two (the two-coloured ribbon) is water-resistant, but can be smoothed with lightly oiled, polished tools. It is much more ductile and can be pulled and stretched until quite thin. Loctite used to sell a product like this in the UK called Handy Strip, but it is no longer available. They still sell something similar in the USA, however, and I now buy mine from there; it is called Duro Master Mend Epoxy. Other epoxy putties are available, but you would have to try them out to see if they had the correct working properties – many of the ones I have tried set too fast. I use the ribbon epoxy putty to form eye rings and leg tufts, and to cover and model the flesh on wire legs. It can also be used to hide the glue line at the neck when necessary. Because it is so ductile it can be drawn out into the texturing, blending in undetectably when painted.

ABRASIVES

There is an extremely wide range of abrasives available now and I often see inexperienced carvers wasting time and temper trying to achieve a good finish with poor ones. The best abrasives that I have used for three-dimensional carving work are the thin, cloth-backed, coated aluminium oxide tapes, which are available in 1 and 4in (25 and 102mm) widths. Paper-backed abrasives fall apart, sometimes in seconds, leaving you with a handful of bits. Most of the glasspaper sold for decorators is only any good for budgerigars; its abrasive quality is usually poor and the grit often comes away altogether!

The cloth-backed aluminium oxide tapes are sold in industrially sized and, unfortunately, industrially priced rolls, and cannot be found easily on the high street. However, many good tool shops, especially woodturners' suppliers, are now selling them by the metre. They are very economical – I use a 1in (25mm) wide strip and only need a few inches per carving on average. A good range of grit sizes are available, from 60–320 grit, so a few metres won't break the bank!

For a finer finish, I use wet-and-dry paper, which is readily available in up to 600 grit, but which, unfortunately, falls to pieces – I haven't been able to find a finer cloth-backed abrasive than 320 grit. I now use Scotchbrite material quite a lot; cut into circular pads and mounted on an arbor in my flexible shaft carver, it achieves a silky-smooth finish.

When carving individual feathers, it is very useful to have some form of semi-rigid sanding strip to make the job easier. Emery boards used for manicuring nails are useful, and can be cut off to give a fresh piece of abrasive as they wear at the end. However, they vary tremendously in quality and many use very poor abrasives. I have used a flexible file made from two strips of Sandvik Sandplate stuck back-to-back, for the past five years and it works very well. I am not sure what the abrasive is, but the surface of the plate is covered in raised concentric circles, and it is available as a self-adhesive or Velcro-backed sheet for use on orbital sanders. A similar flexible, metal sanding plate, but covered with fine, random, tungsten carbide particles, is produced by the Permagrit company and can be cut up to make flexible files, or glued to shaped pieces of wood to form specially shaped riffler tools.

Fig 3.5 Cloth-backed aluminium oxide abrasives are perfect for the carver. This home-made bow sander is excellent for getting blemish-free curved surfaces.

CHAPTER 4

DESIGN AND PLANNING

The purpose of this chapter is to help carvers be aware of the factors influencing overall design and composition – more detailed ideas can be found from many sources. One of the most helpful areas to investigate how best to design a carving is the discipline of flower arranging, and its influence can be seen in many of the better American carvings. Flower arrangers make good use of all the principles of composition, and reading a few books on the subject may well improve your carvings!

In many carvings it is obvious that the subject of the carving has been conceived, and the work carried out, without any real thought being given to its final presentation. You can see such work at competitions or displays; competently carved and painted birds perched on lumps of wood brought straight from the log pile. The proud carver, having achieved their goal of carving the subject, has paid scant attention to the aesthetics of its presentation. One reason for this might be that the carver moved on from decoys where a base did not need to be considered, but bear in mind, it is the finished piece as a whole that is seen by the average viewer, and it is the whole that will be judged, not the details. This is not just true of carving – exactly the same thing may be seen at art exhibitions, where good paintings and drawings are displayed in the cheapest of ready-made frames, detracting from and devaluing the work they contain. This need not happen if consideration is given to a complete design, and all aspects are considered from the planning stage.

To many viewers, especially non-carvers, the overall impression of the carving is probably more important than the standard of workmanship embodied in it. The piece will generally be viewed at a reasonable distance, and what makes it 'good' then is how well it works in terms of overall shape, colour and presence. In fact, a slightly second-rate carving, boldly and well displayed, will probably catch the eye better than an ill-conceived base carrying a technically excellent carving. Remember, the carving is only one part of the composition, and the general viewer, who is not into the technicalities of its production, looks at the completed piece as a whole.

Carved birds, with the exception of decoys, are very rarely freestanding, and the base used to display them needs careful thought if it is to add to the carving rather than detract from it. It is very difficult to carve a bird and then produce a good marriage to a mount afterwards. Found objects such as branches, must be obtained before finalizing the stance of the bird, if they are to fit comfortably in the composition. Wholly man-made bases could be conceived separately, but they are more likely to work well together if they are developed together. To be really successful, even the simplest of bases need to be well planned, and to receive as much care and attention as the carvings themselves.

For a successful overall composition, two basic rules to follow through the development of a plan are:

1 make the subject as interesting, animated and alive as possible; and

2 ensure that the base is sympathetic with, and complementary to the subject.

PLANNING

If you have started to carry out some basic species research (*see* Chapter 5), you will probably already have visualized various possibilities for carvings. You may even have found an interesting piece of driftwood that immediately suggested the subject that should be mounted on it. All that remains is to develop one of these ideas into a well-planned carving.

SUBJECT

Birds do not have one set shape – their appearance is constantly changing with mood and activity. To give life to the carving the subject must either interact directly with the viewer, or else with something contained within the composition, so that the viewer is purely an observer of the interaction. The overall shape and pose of the subject is very important to the action, as it gives visual clues as to what the bird is doing or thinking. An interesting pose can have all the qualities required to capture the attention of the viewer with the most minimalist of bases. Found bases tend to influence the subject, which has to be carved to fit into its surroundings. Making the base from scratch means that you can more easily control the mounting style, which can then be used to complement the pose and accentuate the lines of the subject, or to help draw attention to the action. You have more control of the overall image with a base you created completely yourself.

BASE

Bases for bird carvings seem to take one of two forms; sculptural or naturalistic. In their extreme these may be a rectangular block of wood or stone forming a plinth, or a complete miniature environment of earth, stone, water, wood and plantlife. Initially, the trend was to produce very detailed naturalistic bases to go with detailed carving, but as realistic bird carving has matured in the USA, there has been a shift towards more sculptural or very simple naturalistic bases which place more emphasis on the carving itself.

We tend to think of shape as being solid – self-contained within the subject – but from an artistic point of view, that solid shape influences, and is complemented by

the area about the subject, often called negative space. This space around and between shapes can be very important in the success of a carving. The line of the bird may be mirrored by the branch for instance, so that the eye follows through to the subject and the space contained between the subject and the branch. Open spaces within a composition draw the eye. If you have ever viewed the sculptures of Henry Moore, you will know that your eye is drawn to the scene through the holes which pierce many of his sculptures, and his group sculptures are excellent examples of the use of negative or surrounding space.

Some bird carvings, usually decoys, are made to sit on a table or shelf with no attempt to separate the carving from the environment in which it is placed, not even a simple plinth. Occasionally they may be seen displayed in some form of semi-natural setting in the style of museum taxidermy, but how the decoy carving is viewed is normally left to the owner. It may be displayed alone, giving it prominence, or lost in clutter. It takes a carving with very strong presence to demand its own space.

When including a plinth, or arranging your carving on a branch or with rocks, grass etc., you make your carving part of a larger composition. You have gained more control of how the carving is being displayed, and of the importance of the subject within the overall composition, and if you have succeeded with your design, you will hopefully also influence the owner of the carving to display it well. By controlling how your carving is presented, you can make sure that it gets the prominence it deserves, and catches the viewer's eye – this is most important if you want to catch the judge's eye in competitions. Remember that you are working in three dimensions, so your final composition of base and subject needs to look equally good from any angle.

COMPOSITION

As soon as you attach your carved bird to a rock or twig you have created a more or less

fixed composition, so you should first give
proper thought to what makes a composition good or bad. Good composition is
ruled by the same principles that apply to
painting, graphics, and flower arranging.
Various underlying factors to be considered
when assessing composition include:

- Design
- Scale
- Balance
- Harmony
- Repetition
- Rhythm
- Focus
- Unity
- Texture

All these aspects interact with each other
and good composition achieves a balance of

Fig 4.1 Clay
maquettes or
cardboard cut-outs
can be used to try
out the composition,
especially when
using found bases.

them all, with the emphasis of each varying
from one composition to another. The four
dominant factors in the composition of any
bird carving are design, scale, balance and
focus.

DESIGN
The design is the basic visualization of the
piece; the choice of subject, its activity, how
it is going to be presented, what materials
will be used, how it will be viewed etc.

SCALE
Scale is the size relationship between the
various parts of the composition. This must
take into account other factors like final
siting, and that rather nebulous but closely
linked quality, proportion.

BALANCE
Balance is the relationship between the
visual weight of various parts of the
composition. Balance of form is achieved by
conveying the visual impression of equal
weight about a centre line, but this doesn't
necessarily mean actual symmetry. Balance
is also applicable to the visual effects of
colour and of light and dark.

FOCUS
Focus is the visual, though not necessarily
the actual centre of the composition, and
may concentrate on a particular feature or
an action within the composition.

You can list the factors to be considered,
but there are no hard and fast rules that you
can refer to when working with them on a
composition. You may wish to contrast a
small, brightly coloured bird with a large
expanse of neutral coloured habitat, or
throw your subject deliberately off-balance
to instil a sense of movement; many ideas
could be seen as breaking the rules, but they
may be highly successful! How you assess
these factors is purely subjective, and
probably the best test is whether the piece
'looks right' or 'looks wrong' at first glance.
The most important lesson is to know and
consider the rules, and to be critical with
your own composition and design before
anybody else gets the chance!

PROPORTION

There is a useful rule of proportion called the golden section or golden mean. This rule dates back to the Greek mathematician Euclid, and has been used by artists and sculptors ever since. It is the division of a line such that the shorter section is to the longer section as the longer section is to the whole, and the ratio works out at 0.618:1, or approximately 5:8. Nobody knows why this ratio should work so well, but it occurs frequently in nature, and compositions which use it do have that 'looks right' factor. The golden section can be used for such a deceptively simple decision as 'how large should the base be to balance the height of the carving?'.

Fig 4.2 Simple curlew carved in the decoy style, using antique pine from old warehouse roof beams.

Fig 4.3 My very first attempt, a traditional decoy, displaying all the typical beginners' faults.

CHAPTER 5

CREATING DRAWINGS AND PATTERNS

Carvers of realistic birds require very detailed drawings and as much visual and physical information on the species as possible. Most carvers start with ducks because of the multitude of patterns and carving guides available, mostly from the USA. Some of these are not very accurate, and are suitable only for stylized carvings, but many are very well researched and full of accurate information. If you wish to carve other varieties of bird however, only a handful of books are available, even in the USA, and these cover species which are nearly all American and not found in the British Isles or Europe. This book contains a limited range of drawings, but ready-made drawings for carving British and European species are virtually non-existent, leaving the aspiring carver of British birds to carry out much of their own research.

Many carvers will have a particular favourite species that they want to carve, and it is most unlikely that someone will already have sketched and published a drawing for it, so the ability to produce your own drawings from scratch, or to amend what information is available, becomes essential to get your project off the ground.

Producing your own drawings and patterns is really the first step in taking full artistic, as well as technical control of your work. Slavish imitations of other people's work have their place in the learning process, but once the craft skills have been mastered, you should be ready to take complete control of the whole process, including the research, the drawing and the carving design.

Beginners to realistic carving can now progress very rapidly to a high degree of carving competence with the aid of

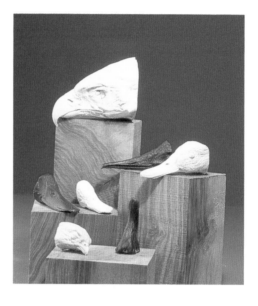

Fig 5.1 Study bills cast from dead birds are available for some species – mainly ducks, geese and birds of prey.

published patterns, books on techniques, and castings of bills and bird carvings by American carvers. Many feel unable to work without these ready-made aids, but originality can be stifled by lack of confidence in working without these props, so have a go at producing your own drawings – it is not as difficult as you might think.

Fig 5.2 Study birds cast from original carvings by several American carvers; these are useful when learning carving and painting techniques.

INITIAL RESEARCH

Thorough research and a good working knowledge of your subject are essential for the successful carving of any subject matter in any style – this does not just apply to birds. The necessary knowledge cannot be instantly acquired, so it pays to be thinking about future projects long before you are likely to want to start carving them.

Start up reference files for all the birds which interest you; collecting all the information is a slow job and the earlier you get started the better. I have got files running on about 500 species – more than I will ever carve in my lifetime, but when someone comes along and commissions a bird which I haven't carved before, then at least I have a good start on the research.

If possible, spend time observing your chosen species, making working sketches and notes, and taking photographs if you have the equipment. Watch videos and make sketches from them as well, look at taxidermy specimens in museums and don't forget to take that all important notebook and sketchpad! Collect magazine photographs, postcards etc., and put them in your reference files too. Check your own reference books for pictures and information, and visit the library.

REFERENCE FILES

Your file should contain anything you can find including:

PUBLISHED PICTURES Cut these from newspapers, magazines and leaflets. I find that it is better to cut out the ones that interest me rather than have to wade through great piles of magazines, trying to find something of use and probably missing the best ones in the process.

SKETCHES If you can draw reasonably well then you can often highlight the details you are interested in which are less obvious in photographs. Sketching and tracing off videos is also quite useful.

POSTCARDS Again, quite a good range of subjects are depicted in postcards and

greetings cards; even cards which are not printed from photographs are worth keeping, but be careful not to duplicate any mistakes perpetrated by the original artist, and don't copy other artists' work, only use it for ideas and reference.

PHOTOGRAPHS Taking photographs of most birds is a time-consuming pastime in its own right, but you can buy prints from bird photographers, and some birds, for example birds of prey, are very easy to photograph at bird centres.

FEATHERS Moulted feathers can often be found, collected from roosting sites, bird parks or even when just out for a walk. If you can accurately identify the donor, then they become a useful addition to your file.

Fig 5.3 Collect as much species-specific information as you can before you start drawing or carving.

Fig 5.4 Study, or cabinet skins can be found in many museums.

BIBLIOGRAPHY List the names of reference books you have found information and pictures in, along with page numbers and a brief description of what is there. This will be a very useful aid at a later date when you want to know which book to borrow from the library again. Also add to the list any references to video footage of your subject, with the position on the tape if your VCR will allow it – you don't want to watch three hours of TV to find that really good twenty second sequence!

VIDEO TAPES Videos are a marvellous substitute for being able to go out and view the bird in the field. Somebody has already found that good viewpoint and edited out the poor shots, leaving just the best footage for you to view. There is a good range of pre-recorded videos available now, covering many of the more interesting species, and there are excellent TV wildlife programmes to tape for future reference. The freeze-frame facility is invaluable for making sketches, as unless you are carving birds of prey, very few birds will stay still long enough to sketch – not for me anyway! Add the details of your tape contents to your bibliography.

RESEARCHING CHARACTERISTICS AND HABITAT

Read as much as possible about your chosen bird for an insight into its characteristic behaviour patterns and preferred habitats.

When you combine this with actually spending time watching your subject, either in the flesh or on video, you will get a feeling for the bird's natural characteristics of shape, action, colour etc. – the overall impression of the bird which ornithologists call 'Jizz'. Getting a feeling for your subject in this way will be a great help later, when you come to critically examine your drawing, maquette or carving.

RESEARCHING DIMENSIONS

Having filled your file with all the information you can find, and with your head buzzing with the Jizz (I always think that sounds like an insect) you have only one thing missing before you begin to draw – some actual known dimensions. Now, if you are carving the yellow-bellied, white-rumped toad eater of Sumatra, you will have an advantage over almost everyone looking at your work; you're the expert and you will not find many prepared to say 'That's wrong' or 'It can't do that'. However, if you get a common garden bird even a little wrong, the whole world seems to know more than you. No amount of waffle or excuses like 'actually it's the subspecies giganticus' will work. You need to get it right to keep your credibility, and adequate information is the key!

Unfortunately for the squeamish, actually getting close enough to a bird to measure it usually means it is, like the parrot in the Monty Python sketch, deceased. Not only will it have ceased to be, but it is quite likely to have been mangled by the cat or the traffic, and may even be starting to decompose! I will start with the more pleasant options for finding dimensions.

Many field guides will give a size for a bird, and possibly a wingspan. Un-fortunately, the size refers to the bill tip to tail tip length, with bird stretched out in the 'playing dead' position – not a generally useful pose. If this is all you can find though, it can be used to give some approximate dimensions, especially if the bird has a definite neck. The tail to breast length can be added to the neck, and the beak tip to spine length to find the approximate scale of a photograph, though while this may work tolerably well on a large bird, it is not very accurate on small birds. Full wingspan measurements are also often given, but these are only of real use if you are doing outstretched wings. What you really want is the wing cord measurement (wing tip to wrist), which is much more useful. You are really looking for dimensions of beaks, tails, wings, and feet, and for feather size and shape etc.

Measurements are taken using the bill tip and the ends of the tail and wings as reference points for the dimensions which could be termed 'fixed'. It is better to measure several specimens of similar maturity and average the measurements to create your 'ideal bird'. Suitably tame, captive or recuperating birds may allow themselves to be measured, but only do this with an experienced handler to prevent over stressing the bird. If you know any bird ringers you should be able to get some information from them, as they usually measure and weigh birds when they catch them. Ringers' handbooks are full of useful and very detailed information about birds and are worth checking out, but for anything else you need to go back to the bird that 'has ceased to be'.

The most pleasant dead birds to handle and measure are those which have come via the taxidermist rather than the cat or the roadside. These are usually made into either full mounts or study skins (also known as cabinet skins). You will not necessarily have to purchase these – you might know someone with a mount, or you could try a local museum which will probably have quite a few. Some museums have very large collections of both mounts and skins, and an enquiry at your local museum should put you in touch with the nearest collection. Access arrangements vary with each museum, and at some you will have to examine skins in the museum, while at others they may be lent out for a short time like library books.

Taxidermy mounts should not be relied upon for the overall shape of a subject –

Fig 5.5 Taxidermy is not always reliable – who strangled the mallard?

badly prepared birds can be quite distorted in both size and shape. Good photographs together with a knowledge of the Jizz of your subject are necessary to get a good representative shape and pose.

When handling taxidermy specimens do not smoke or eat, and make sure you wash your hands thoroughly; this is good hygiene practice with any mount, but many older specimens were preserved using dangerous chemicals like arsenic, so with them these rules become much more important.

If the specimen has to be examined at the museum, then detailed reference notes and sketches should be made. Prepare beforehand, a chart to record all the key dimensions, and make measured sketches of the bill, and of feather shape, size and layout. This chart will become an invaluable reference source, used in all stages of drawing and carving. Make colour notes if the specimen is suitable, using either a colour reference system (*see* Colour reference system in Chapter 10, on page 75), or mixing paints up to match, keeping accurate notes on the colour mixes. Don't just record the main colours – look for hints of other colours showing up when caught by the light, and examine feather tips for colour edging. It may save some time if you have tried to create the colours from photographs beforehand, so that you are looking to fine-tune the mixes rather than starting from scratch.

The least pleasant way of collecting your data is from the bird the cat brought in, or that you picked up at the side of the road. It is possible to preserve such specimens by DIY taxidermy, and learning the skills to prepare a study skin only takes a couple of days; the real skill of the taxidermist is in making the skins into mounted birds. However, I prefer to carefully wrap and bag the specimen and deep freeze it to kill off parasites and as many disease organisms as possible before taking measurements and then burying the corpse. It is possible to keep feather samples from the corpse, for shape and colour reference, and even preserving a wing is not too difficult, providing the muscles are removed from the leading edge before treating with Borax and thoroughly drying. Full instructions for this, and for the production of your own cabinet skins, is included in John C Metcalf's *Taxidermy,* details of which are listed in Recommended reading on page 160. I only collect specimens that are fresh, at all times handle them wearing surgical rubber gloves, and I am scrupulous about hygiene.

By now you should be getting very familiar with your subject and be looking with a 'seeing eye', which is very different from just watching. Now you are really ready to commence the first stages in making your own drawings and patterns.

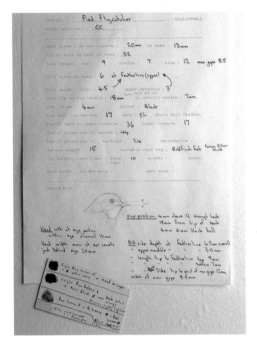

Fig 5.6 Keep notes of the dimensions and colours obtained from study skins.

Fig 5.7 Simple taxidermy will enable you to preserve your own specimens like these.

Fig 5.8 Get better specimens professionally mounted, preferably in a pose you would want to carve.

ALTERING PUBLISHED PATTERNS

Even if you intend to carve a published pattern as it is supplied, to get the best results, some research on your part is still necessary, as a drawing cannot tell you everything about the subject. You need to become as familiar as possible with the bird you wish to carve and to collect as much reference material as you can to refer to whilst carving. Whenever I carve a particular species, I am surrounded by photographs, notes, and sketches, even if I am working from a drawing that I prepared.

The first, easy step in creating your own, original work, is to take the groundwork already provided by a published pattern, and alter it to your personal requirements. You can quickly re-pose the subject without having to do all the initial research, although you are, of course, relying on the original draughtsman's information being correct.

Assuming you have a good original pattern, there are many simple alterations which may be carried out – you will only need a little time spent studying the live subject, or photographs from your reference file to spot suitable modifications.

Alterations will give a published design your own personal stamp, and increase your personal pleasure in the carving created.

Simply redrawing the head in a different position and blending the neckline back into the body, or tilting the head to the side, will give a totally different look. Here are some of the possibilities for simple modifications to published realistic patterns. All are relevant to decoys, and most are applicable to other styles of carving as well.

HEAD AND NECK

1 Rotate the head slightly to get away from that straight ahead, 'wooden' decoy look; it instantly adds more life.

2 The neck can be raised, pulled down or extended forward, and this will alter the mood of the bird. Generally, the head is raised when the bird is alert, and lowered when it is relaxed. The neck extended fully forward with the bill open is an aggressive stance, but could be adapted into a feeding one, especially if combined with some tilt of the head axis to one side.

3 Tilting the head over to one side, making one eye higher than the other, will give an inquisitive look to the bird.

4 The bill can be opened to signify aggression, feeding or calling.

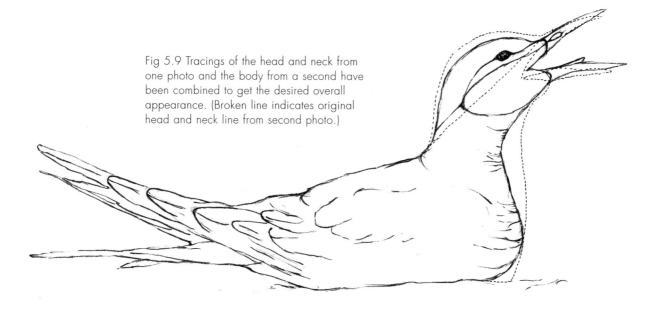

Fig 5.9 Tracings of the head and neck from one photo and the body from a second have been combined to get the desired overall appearance. (Broken line indicates original head and neck line from second photo.)

TAIL

1 Raising or lowering the tail can alter the mood of the bird.

2 Tail feathers can be spread or closed, totally altering the shape of the tail area.

3 The rump can be turned, putting the centre line of the tail at an angle to the body.

WINGS

1 Wings can be held high above the back, laid flat along the body, or trailed low. If you have sufficient information, a much more ambitious pose would be a partial or full, open-winged pose, but don't create a flying plank – birds wings aren't flat!

2 The wing tips may be crossed or uncrossed above the tail area when held at rest.

BODY

1 In a waterline carving of waterfowl, the angle of the bird to the water surface may be altered to lower or raise the breast or rump. In the case of full-bodied birds, altering the angle of the body to the legs will change the whole shape of the composition.

Wherever possible, study live birds, or at least photographs, to establish a pose that looks natural and not contrived; beware of making a bird too contorted without having sufficient information on how the move-ments affect the rest of the body shape: the preening and sleeping positions of birds change their overall body shape quite dramatically. Study your subject for courtship and other behavioural patterns as well, as these can make good poses for your work.

When you have finished altering a pattern look hard and long at your new drawing; if it doesn't look right on paper, transferring it to wood is not going to improve it! If it looks good, try making a clay maquette, or power carve a quick rough in jelutong (at a reduced scale if necessary) before you commence your final carving, just to make sure.

Fig 5.10 The dimensions taken from study skins are transferred onto the basic drawing which was created from photographic information.

CREATING DRAWINGS FROM SCRATCH

Bird drawings cannot be approached in quite the same fashion as an engineering drawing, as there are no flat planes, fixed datum points or precise shapes. These factors may seem to make the task almost impossible, but with a planned, logical approach to the work, they can be fairly easily overcome.

Good, accurate drawings are as essential to the carving of a realistic bird as is the idea for the overall concept or design. The most important aspect of producing worthwhile drawings is thorough research; collect and study as much information as possible before charging ahead.

DRAWING EQUIPMENT

You don't need access to any fancy equipment to produce your drawing; a technical drawing pencil with a 0.5mm, 2H lead, disposable drawing pens with 0.1 and 0.5mm tips, a ruler, and dividers or measuring callipers, an eraser and a pad of 90gsm tracing paper will prove ideal.

I usually produce a general drawing for a species rather than one particular pose as this can then be used as the basis for patterns for many different carvings of the same species. The patterns used for the final carvings can be made with simple adjust-ments in the same way as alterations to commercial patterns are done, or by doing a complete redraw, using a different overall body shape, with the earlier details superimposed on it. This is one of the reasons that I use tracing paper for my drawings, it enables me to quickly transfer details from one drawing to another.

THE STARTING POINT – GENERAL SHAPE

The drawing is started by sketching the overall shape of the bird onto the paper. I look for what I feel is a typical overall shape for that species. This may come from a sketch or a good photograph that conveys the general characteristics of the subject.

The overall shape and bulk of a small bird can vary immensely, and is affected by environmental factors like cold, wind and rain, or emotional factors such as aggression and fear. The sleek nuthatch scurrying down a tree in midsummer, may become a ping pong ball with a beak in a harsh winter woodland environment – both may make interesting carvings but neither would be typical of the familiar shape and bulk of the bird when more 'average' conditions prevail. The drawing you choose to produce may be general purpose or pose specific, but good photographs or sketches will still form its core. Your knowledge of the subject and its Jizz will help in the selection of suitable photographs, avoiding obvious photographic distortions. Photographs can then be brought to full scale, manually or with a photocopier, and you can trace the parts you want.

It is unlikely that you will find just what you want in one photograph, and anyway, you may be infringeing someone's copyright if you do. Because camera angles often make pictures rather distorted, combine the best elements from several photographs to form a suitable, undistorted, composite image. Access to a photocopier with the ability to vary scale is invaluable when working with different photographs, although you can rescale them manually using a squared grid or a pantograph. The bill tip to eye centre, and wing cord measurements are the most useful when trying to assess and adjust the scale of a photograph or drawing, and with a photocopier and ruler you will quickly get what you need. In the absence of a photocopier, the simplest and cheapest method is to trace the outline of the photograph onto a squared grid, and then to prepare a second squared grid with proportionately larger or smaller squares, onto which the tracing can be redrawn square by square. A pantograph could also be used if you have or can make one, and someone once told me how to scale a drawing using an elastic band, although I don't think the results would be very consistent!

The various elements, which, hopefully, are now all drawn at the same scale, on individual pieces of tracing paper, are lightly traced onto the main drawing sheet to act as the core element of the drawing. Be critical of the overall shape and bulk at this stage — it is too late to decide that the head is too small when you are half way through the carving!

THE HEAD

The basic drawing is now refined using the details from the data you have gathered. I like to draw the details onto separate pieces of tracing paper first; these can then be arranged under the main drawing sheet, allowing the relative positions of the various elements to be adjusted, before being traced onto the final drawing. These various part drawings are kept, to be used again for 'posed' drawings if required.

I usually start by detailing the bill and eye area. The head will be the focal point of the carving, so it is important to get this area looking correct from the start. The following dimensions are those which are used when detailing the drawing (*see* Fig 5.11). It is impossible to always determine exact dimensions, and many measurements will be empirical, or at best a good average.

(a) Beak tip to eye centre (averaged from measurements taken on both sides of the head).

(b) Beak tip to nostril centre (and the length of nostril if it is a large bill).

(c) Beak length along the top (measured to the feather line).

(d) Beak length at the side (measured to the feather line).

(e) Beak length along the bottom (measured to the feather line).

(f) Maximum gape (maximum width at the back of the beak, behind the feather line, where the corner of the mouth lies).

(g) Total beak depth (at feather line, upper and lower mandibles with the beak closed).

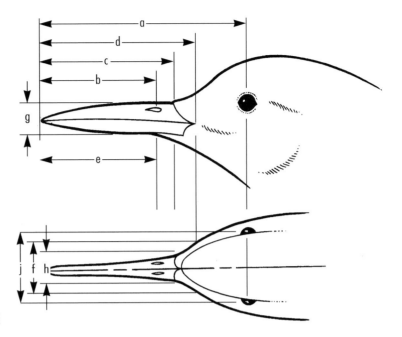

Fig 5.11 Head dimensions used in detailing.

(h) Maximum beak width (at feather line; this is not the same as the gape).

(i) Upper mandible depth (at feather line; not marked on diagram).

(j) Eye to eye distance (measured at the front of the eye socket).

(k) Maximum width of skull (measured over the feathers; not marked on diagram).

EYE

Determining the eye position on the head is done visually, studying live birds and photographs. Look particularly at the eye's relationship to a line drawn along the bottom edge of the upper mandible and the distance from the top of the head (*see* Fig 5.12). Take great care to get the eye correctly placed, not too near the top or

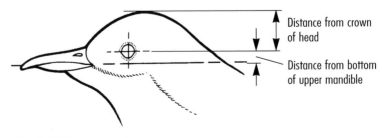

Fig 5.12 Positioning the eye.

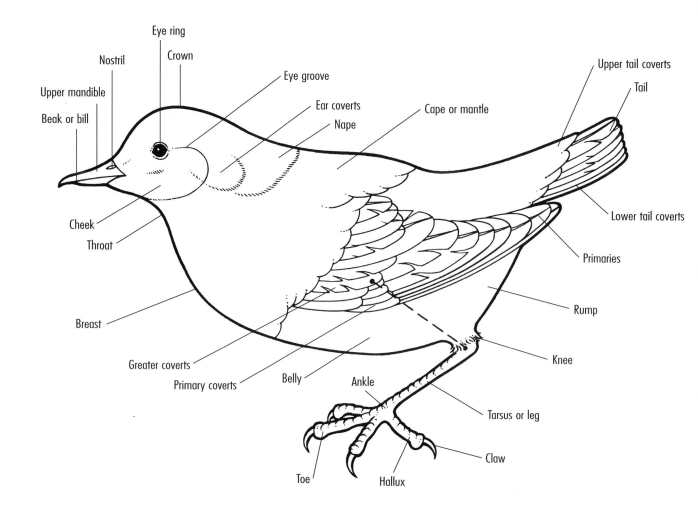

Eye ring
Crown
Nostril
Upper mandible
Beak or bill
Eye groove
Ear coverts
Nape
Cape or mantle
Upper tail coverts
Tail
Cheek
Throat
Lower tail coverts
Primaries
Breast
Rump
Greater coverts
Knee
Primary coverts
Belly
Ankle
Tarsus or leg
Claw
Toe
Hallux

Fig 5.13
Topography of a
typical bird.

front of the head, or in line with the beak opening. The eye sits in a channel between the cheek and the crown, and the most important dimension is the eye to eye distance at the front of the eye socket within this channel (*see* Fig 5.11; *see also* Fig 5.12). The width of the head at the crown and cheek (above and below the eye channel), and the shape of the crown, are all dependent upon the feathers and cannot be measured, however, studying suitable photographs will enable you to make a good estimate based on the skull width measurement.

Eye sizes and colour charts can be obtained from a taxidermists' reference book, or from the glass eye suppliers.

BEAK

Once you have resolved the position of the eye, you can start to draw in a more accurate bill (*see* Figs 5.12 and 5.13). Using

the bill tip to eye centre measurement, (a), to find the end of the bill, draw in the line running through the lower edge of the upper mandible, which you observed when positioning the eye, making sure that it leaves the head at the correct angle. The upper mandible is effectively fixed to the skull, so it always joins the skull at much the same angle; in most species only the jaw and lower mandible move. Now use the upper mandible depth, (i), and overall bill depth measurement, (g), to form two small rectangular boxes above and below this line. The correctly shaped beak profile can now be drawn within the confines of these two boxes, and the nostril measurement, (b), can be transferred to the drawing. Pay particular attention to the shape formed where the bill meets the feather line. Cross sectional drawings and sketches of any ridges or marks which the bill exhibits should be made if possible, to aid in the correct shaping of the bill later. If an open mouth drawing is required, remember that the jaw is hinged well back on the skull, behind the eyes; you cannot just open the bill where it meets the feather line or the angle of the lower mandible will look completely wrong.

The upper mandible and eye positions are fixed in relation to each other by the skull, and the eye to eye distance is similarly held, so it follows that if these measurements are accurately applied to the carving of a good profile, a well-formed head should result. Many beginners' carvings are marred by too widely spaced eyes, and over-sized bills. Although these dimensions are tied together, the overall head size and shape is made up of feathers and influenced by environment and emotion; typical head shapes do vary from species to species though. The overall head width is variable, but is never going to be less than the measurement of maximum skull width, (k), on a taxidermy specimen. Generally, the widest part of the head is going to be the cheek area below and slightly behind the eye, and the crown above the eye groove is going to be somewhat narrower than the cheek.

Having redrawn the eye and beak areas on the main profile drawing, a second copy can be made with feather details drawn on, particularly the flow lines of feathers across the surface, as the individual feathers on most small birds' heads are hairy and indistinct.

Fig 5.14 Feather flow on the head of a great spotted woodpecker: spiky 'whiskers' stick out around the bill.

TAIL AREA

The tail usually receives my attention next. As you can record very little detail on the profile view, I often prepare secondary upper and lower tail surface drawings as part of the plan view, the upper surface view usually combined with the plan view unless it is obscured by the wings. The following dimensions are obtained and transferred to the main drawing (*see* Fig 5.15; *see also* Fig 5.13).

(a) Longest tail feather tip to shortest tail feather tip.

(b) Tip of longest feather to upper tail coverts.

(c) Tip of longest tail feather to lower tail coverts.

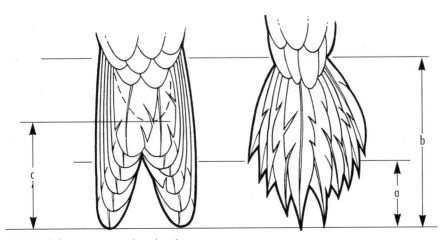

Fig 5.15 Tail dimensions used in detailing.

The measurement for the tip of longest tail feather to tip of longest wing feather can also be used, though this is only of any value if you are duplicating a taxidermy pose, as the measurement varies greatly with the wings held differently.

WINGS

Measurements are taken from the tip of the longest primary feather on a folded wing. Study how the various feather groups are laid out. Wing topography is quite complex, and not all feather groups show up on different species of bird. The relative size and shape of the groups differ with wing size and shape, and some groups may be hidden by body contour feathers covering part of the wing. (*See* Fig 5.16). It is, hardly surprisingly, the most complex area of feathers on the bird and not all that easy to follow. The relative sizes and relationships of the groups of feathers vary slightly from species to species. This depends upon the wing shape, which alters to cope with different birds' flying styles and habitat.

Unless you have a freshly dead specimen rather than a taxidermist's one, it is not possible to open the wing to draw it. I prepare my own study skins with one wing spread, but museum skins are not done this way as they take up too much room and are liable to damage. Using some ingenuity to adapt an existing open wing drawing for a bird of similar wing shape and habitat might prove the only practical step. Dried wings of certain species are available as fly-tying materials from angling shops and can be bought for use as reference. Although not much use initially, these can be laid on a wire grid, suspended over damp sawdust, in

Fig 5.17 Wings preserved from found corpses or bought at fishing tackle shops as fly tying material.

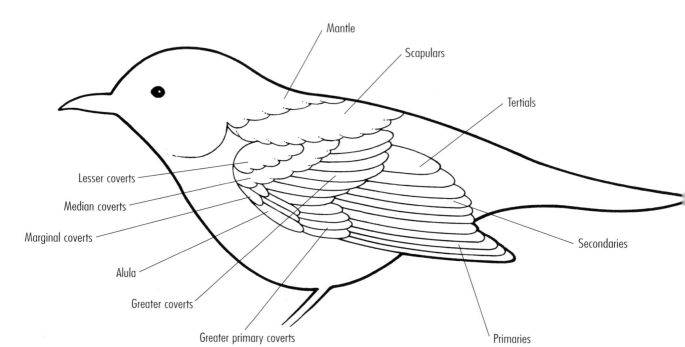

Fig 5.16 Wing topography of a typical small woodland/garden bird. The size, shape and visibility of feather groups will differ from bird to bird.

a sealed plastic cake box for a few days. When they are removed you will find that they have 'relaxed' and can be opened up and pinned out on a piece of cardboard or polystyrene to dry in the open position. A good field guide or ringers' guide can be used to help identify and name the different feather groups, and may even contain drawings of some species.

The principal measurements taken are those shown below, although not all the feather groups will be identifiable on some folded wings (*see* Fig 5.18).

(a) Longest primary feather tip to the tip of each individual primary feather.

(b) Longest primary tip to tip of each individual secondary.

(c) Longest primary tip to each individual tertial tip.

(d) Longest primary tip to the greater primary covert group.

(e) Longest primary tip to the greater covert group.

(f) Longest primary tip to the alula group.

(g) Longest primary tip to the median covert group.

(h) Longest primary tip to the first joint (wing cord measurement, or overall length of the folded wing).

Other measurements may need to be checked as the drawing proceeds. Firstly, decide on the position of the wing tip in relation to the tail, by referring to photographs or observations. Mark the overall length of the folded wing (wing cord) and lightly pencil in the approximate positions of the feather groups. Now, starting from the wing tip and working towards the head, transfer the positions of each individual feather tip, as a short pencil line. Working with one feather group at a time, so that the drawing is not completely covered with transferred dimensions, draw the individual feathers. Several redrafts will probably be required before you get it looking right, but the pencilled lines indicating

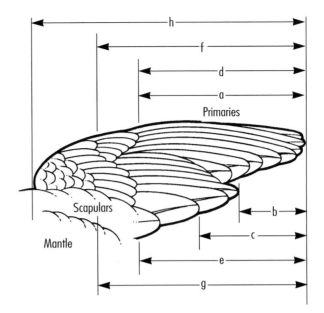

Fig 5.18 Wing dimensions used in detailing.

the feather tip positions make redrawing quite a quick process. Study the feather shapes on the mounted specimen, don't just invent them. The hard-edged feathers which make up the wings and tail have distinctive shapes, but you can use more artistic flair on the soft body contour feathers which, unlike the hard-edged feathers, do not have distinctive outlines. You should, however, check the size and spacing of individual feathers on the chest, cape, side pocket, head, belly, and upper and lower tail coverts: these can be indicated on the drawing or a separate small sketch.

TIDYING UP

Your profile drawing should now be completed; add any notes or additional sketches you think fit, including some detailed sketches and measurements of the legs and feet, although taxidermy specimens are often too dried up and brittle to be of much use. Examine your drawn profile critically – does it look and feel correct? If you are not sure about an area, quickly trace over the drawing onto a fresh sheet of tracing paper and then redraw the offending area, that way you can compare the old version with the new and revert back to it if the new one is not an improvement. When I went back to my working profile of the tern (*see* Fig 5.19), I wasn't happy with the look of the body or the chest, so I cut and

Fig 5.19 Working drawing created from the sketch in Fig 5.9 and information from other sources, including study skins.

adjusted two photocopies of the profile to suit a photograph that showed the look I wanted. I then tidied this profile up to get a final version. When you are completely happy, ink in the drawing and take some photocopies for general workshop use. Store the original in a safe place — it represents a lot of time and effort!

CREATING THE PLAN VIEW

Developing the plan view creates its own set of problems, the answers to which, for some, can often only be solved by experimentation. You are unlikely to be lucky enough to find a photograph which shows anything like a plan view. If you are using a taxidermy mount or cat offering, as opposed to a cabinet skin, then you should be able to get a good idea of the plan view of the body and head; if not, trial and error, based on observation, becomes the order of the day.

The body mass of most small birds is basically egg-shaped, with the wider end forming the breast. You will already have some idea of the minimum head width (the skull width measured over the feathers), so a front view of the bird, which can usually be found, can be examined to check the proportions of body and head widths. Remember that the shape is not a firmly defined one, but a very variable mass of feathers and air, so you are looking for proportion and visual balance to match the profile you have already established. Transfer the major dimensions from the profile drawing in the usual manner, extending parallel lines out from the principal points of the first drawing, onto the new drawing area or sheet. The plan view drawing needs to be prepared at 90° to the profile drawing (*see* Fig 5.21). Again, the drawing is started by lightly sketching the overall shape, and then adding the detail; separate views can be

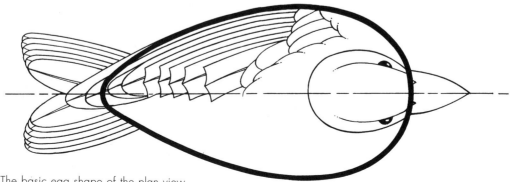

Fig 5.20 The basic egg shape of the plan view.

Fig 5.21 Transferring relative positions to the second view of the drawings.

done for the head and body if required. The tail details are added first, and they need to be closely observed because, like wings, they vary from species to species: shapes vary considerably, with rounded, square, and V-shaped tails all common. Secondary drawings of fully open or closed tails can be prepared at the same time, along with an under tail view, and these are all useful. Tails have an even number of feathers, most commonly 12 or 14, so you should not get a centre feather as often seen on carvings. It is

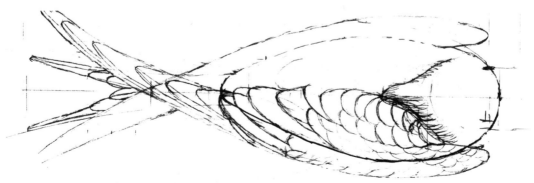

Fig 5.22 Plan view created from the profile drawing in Fig 5.19.

fairly easy to slip a piece of paper between individual tail feathers so that their shapes can be drawn. Note that the position of the quill is not always down the centre of a feather, as many beginners believe!

The tail would often be partially obscured by the wings on many plan views, so it is useful to show one or the other as a dotted area, and to put the detail in a secondary drawing. Alternatively, draw the wing held slightly open to clear the tail area. Don't forget that the tail feathers originate well back on the bird, in the same area as the tail coverts; like icebergs there is a lot hidden! As a simple rule of thumb, don't angle the outside feathers at more than 30° to the body centre-line. You can include more detail if you draw the tail held slightly spread, and the drawing will be less cluttered. When you have drawn the upper surface, trace the outline and use this to create the under tail view.

MAQUETTES

A maquette is a preliminary working model created as part of the design process – I use Plasticine to model mine. They may at first seem like a waste of time and effort, but working in clay or Plasticine, it is easy to

put material back, as well as to take it away, and you can literally get hold of the head and turn it to a different attitude – you can't change the pose on a carving that easily! The maquette can also be viewed from all positions to make sure the carving will look good from every direction and not just have one good side.

If you are carving a bird to fit onto an existing piece of driftwood, a life-size cardboard cut-out can be attached with some Blu-Tack, to check that the scale of the bird and base are compatible, before making a maquette. Again, it is easier to find a new base before you start to carve than to find something suitable later.

When you are happy with the maquette, it can then be traced around to obtain the bandsawing pattern. To do this, fix the model over a piece of card, using blocks if necessary, offer a set square up to the edge of the maquette and put a pencil dot on the card against the base of the set square. Repeat this all around the model, then join up the dots, thus forming the pattern.

Set the model up at exactly 90° to the first drawing and repeat the procedure to get the second profiling pattern. This process is made much easier if the maquette is built on a stand with a square wooden base.

Fig 5.23 Plasticine is useful for creating maquettes of small birds, and plastic sheet or card can be used to form the wings and tail.

Fig 5.24 The finished maquette will save much time when carving.

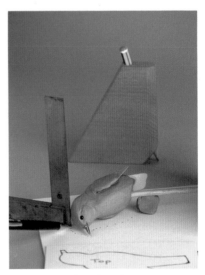

Fig 5.25 Making bandsawing patterns from a maquette: my home-made square with a built-in pencil speeds up the job.

COPYRIGHT AND MORAL RIGHTS

When creating your own drawings, you should be aware that all illustrations and designs, and even photographic images, may be copyright, and you may be infringeing copyright if you copy the work of other artists without their permission. Copyright and moral rights protection is a very complex field, and the following points are to help ensure that carvers do have at least the basic grasp of what it means to them. Please remember that these notes represent the legislation as I understand it, but my interpretation may not be the courts!

COPYRIGHT

1 All original artistic works, and works of artistic craftsmanship, including paintings, drawings, sculpture, carvings, and photographs, carry with them the protection of copyright. This normally belongs to the artist, unless the work was created as part of the duties of employment, in which case the employer would own the copyright.

2 The artist can assign the copyright to another person by a signed document in writing, but owning a work does not automatically mean that you have bought the copyright in the work; that will usually still belong to the person who created it.

3 Owning the copyright normally gives you the exclusive rights to authorize or to make copies or adaptations of the work, unless these rights have already been granted to someone else.

4 Only works first published in the UK or another qualifying country, or created by a 'qualifying person' (such as a British citizen) will be protected by the Copyright Designs and Patents Act 1988. This means that copying a foreign artist, or your work being copied abroad, may well be an infringement of copyright not only in the country where it originated, but also where it was copied, if the country where it was copied is (like the UK) a member of one of the international copyright conventions, such as the Berne or UCC Conventions (most developed countries now are).

5 Even if someone commissions you to create a carving, you automatically retain the copyright of the work if it was created after August 1989. The position may be different for pre-1989 commissioned works.

6 Copyright comes into force automatically when the work is created (which means substantially finished), and does not need to be registered.

7 You don't need to use the © symbol in the UK, but its use is still required in some UCC Convention countries, and is still recommended as a reminder to others. The copyright notice required by the UCC is: © [name of copyright owner] [year of first publication], for example, © David Tippey 1996.

8 At the time of writing, copyright in artistic works throughout the EU lasts for 70 years from the end of the year in which the artist dies. Most moral rights last for the same length of time.

9 A signed written agreement is required to assign the copyright to another person or organization, unless the artist dies, when it transfers to his estate.

10 The artist may license the copying of any substantial part of his work, and control the number of reproductions made, usually for a fee.

11 Copying and display of another's work without permission is an infringement of copyright.

MORAL RIGHTS

1 Moral rights are to protect the artist and his work, giving him (amongst other things) the right to be identified as the creator of the work when it is displayed (authorship), and to help prevent adverse treatment of the work (integrity). The right to claim authorship (sometimes known as the right of paternity) must be asserted by the artist before it can be exercized.

2 They are designed to prevent others claiming to be the original artist of the work and give the artist the right to object to any derogatory treatment of the work.

3 Moral rights always belong to the artist, or his estate after death, and cannot be assigned to a third party, but they may be waived by a written or verbal agreement.

HOW THEY AFFECT THE AVERAGE CARVER

Again I must point out that this is my interpretation and opinion, totally untested in law, but what I perceive as a fair rendering of the information I have read.

Copies of other artists' work may, in some circumstances, be made without permission, if the intended purpose of the copying was for what is termed 'fair dealing'. This includes limited copying (usually only in single copies) for the purposes of research and private study, and also copying for the purposes of criticism and review (for example in a text book, or an article) provided sufficient acknowledgement is given. This would allow the carver to make a copy of another's work, but exhibiting or selling that copy would almost certainly not count as fair dealing, and would therefore be a copyright infringement. I believe this would also ban other people from entering copies of the work in competitions. Where a design has been published, it depends upon what rights have been granted to the purchaser of the design, but I would certainly welcome labelling of derivative work entered in competitions as, 'After a work by . . .' or 'from an original design by . . .', as being morally and ethically correct. Depending on the standard of the reproduction, your work could also be infringeing the creator's moral rights to be cited as the artist, and to the integrity of his work, if it is shown in public!

I believe that when plans or designs for works, including carvings, are published, anyone may follow those plans or designs in order to make their own versions of the works pictured. The author will still own the copyright in the plans and designs themselves, however, and will have a moral right to be credited as the author (if he asserts it), but he probably grants a limited licence to the purchaser to use the design. The designs incorporated in this book are copyright: they may be used to make your own versions of the works pictured for personal or competition use, but may not be offered for sale.

Photographs are also likely to be copyright works if they have enough 'originality'. Creating an identifiable, three-dimensional version of a two-dimensional work such as a photograph may well be copyright infringement, and also, could be taken as derogatory treatment of the original work, which is why it is wise to base your own designs on several photographs plus additional material. However, I think it is unlikely that basing a carving on one photograph of a wildlife subject would ever be a problem, unless the photograph contained a very obvious and original design element, which was repeated in the three-dimensional version.

CHAPTER 6

THE BLANK

MARKING OUT THE BLANK

Cutting patterns are prepared either from the working drawing or a maquette (*see* Maquettes in Chapter 5, on page 42). Having drawn out the cutting pattern, I usually then create a cardboard pattern to mark out the actual blank. Extra material should be added to the patterns around the beak, tail and wing tips, and because the pattern will be traced around, effectively, a little will be added all around the bird as well, providing that all the cutting is done accurately to be outside the line. If the head is to be 'turned in the block', then a little more material may be needed in the neck area as well.

Choose a block of defect-free timber, then square the edges and plane the surface so that the marking out can be easily seen. If the block is not square, the blank will not be accurately cut and the bandsaw blade may run out of the edge of the block – extremely hazardous for your finger count! The timber needs to be at least ¼in (6mm) larger all round than the maximum dimensions of the pattern, to make reassembly of the block and compound bandsawing easier. Align the patterns and use a pencil or felt-tip pen to trace around them onto the clean, squared timber block.

BANDSAWING

When the patterns for both the side and top profiles have been drawn, the first profile is carefully cut to the outside of the pencil line; this allows just that little extra material all around the bird. Make sure you are using a sharp blade – blunt ones 'run off' and do not cut accurately through the thickness of the timber. The cutting should be done so that the waste pieces from the first profile can be used to form a cradle to support the

blank whilst cutting the second profile. Try to keep the waste as two complete pieces, one of which will already have the second profile drawn on it. Reassemble the blank and the waste into a block, in readiness for sawing out the second profile. The various pieces can be held together with your hands, but for safety, as well as precluding the possibility of the whole lot moving when you start to cut, a few spots of glue from a hot melt glue gun will tack the offcuts firmly in place. Adhesive tape, push pins (map pins) or moulding pins can also be used to hold the bits together, but you run the risk of hitting pins with the bandsaw blade, which won't do much for its working life!

Take the reassembled block back to the bandsaw and cut the second profile carefully, as before. This time, when the offcuts fall away there should be a blocky, square-cornered, but bird-like shape left. You seem to end up with a greater volume of waste than the block you started with, and there is not much you can do with those expensive little pieces of wood, other than use them for kindling, so make sure the cutting is accurate first time. The large offcuts should still retain the line of the actual pattern, and they can be cleaned up to form durable, wooden profile patterns for any subsequent versions of the carving.

I cut the side profile first, mainly out of habit, as that is often the only profile I use. I cut the block to the maximum body width and draw on the top profile directly without making a separate pattern first, but referring to the working drawings. I do this especially if I want to turn the head or tail, in which case I draw these onto the top surface of the cut side profile, using new centre-lines. Whether I use a pattern for the top profile or not, I still use part of the waste from the first profiling to create a cradle to hold the blank firmly whilst I bandsaw the second outline. (*See* Figs 6.3–6.5.)

Fig 6.1 The patterns are aligned and transferred onto the squared timber.

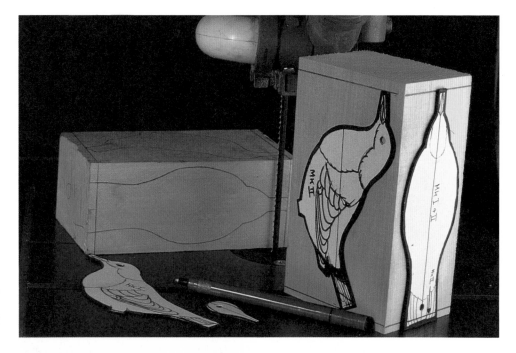

Fig 6.2 After drawing around the patterns for both side and top, the side profile is carefully cut out.

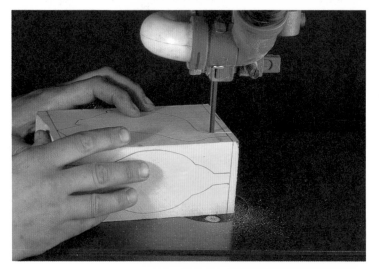

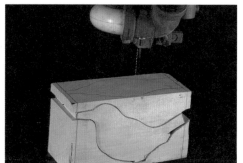

Fig 6.3 The waste pieces from cutting the first profile are used to support the blank, whilst cutting the top view.

Fig 6.4 Using glue from a glue gun to tack the offcuts in place.

Fig 6.5 Cutting the top profile on the reassembled block.

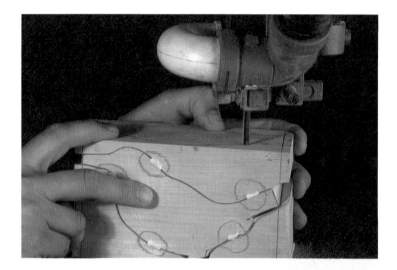

Fig 6.6 The finished carving blank with the large collection of offcuts produced.

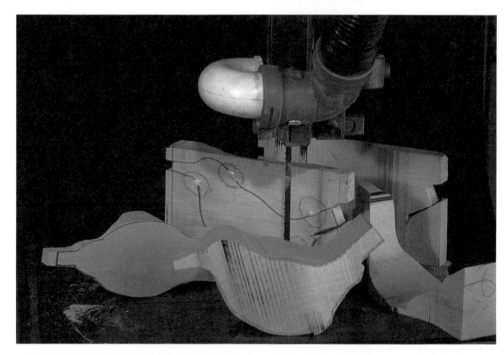

Fig 6.7 Offcuts trimmed to provide durable patterns for future use.

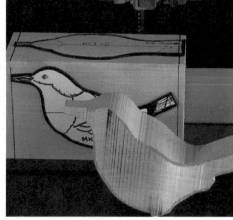

Fig 6.8 The finished carving blank produced from patterns.

ROUGHING OUT A TURNED HEAD

If the head has been turned along a different axis to the body, it creates some interesting problems. (Unless you are experienced in carving, it is simpler to avoid the problems posed by introducing turned heads and tails on your first attempt.) To try and show this

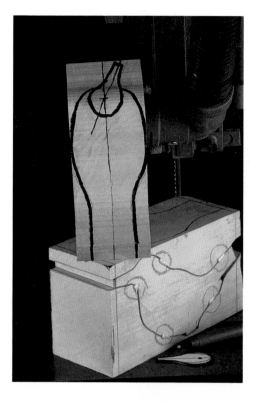

more clearly, I carved 'The Big Dipper', a head and shoulders only version at about twice full size, so that it would show up better in the photographs.

You can see that when viewed along the body centre-line, or from directly above, the head looks perfectly normal. However, when you look down the centre-line of the head, you can see that the profile is strangely distorted, with one side running up to a peak. Drawing a series of lines at right angles to the head's centre-line shows up the problem even better! If you look at the four quarters of the head arrayed along the centre-line, two opposing quadrants are high and two are low. This needs to be fixed before any further work is done, because if the shape cannot be corrected, leaving sufficient material for consequent carving, then the blank will have to be scrapped. When turning the head, it is a good idea to allow some extra timber where it meets the body for profile corrections, especially under the chin, which seems to create more problems than around the back of the neck.

Correction of the head shape is fairly easy if carried out in a logical manner, and the method I use starts with drawing a series of lines at right angles to the centre-line of the head, in the same way as used to illustrate the distortion in the photograph of the Big Dipper.

Fig 6.9 The side profile for the body is marked out as before, but the top profile of the head is drawn along a different centre-line, using a separate pattern.

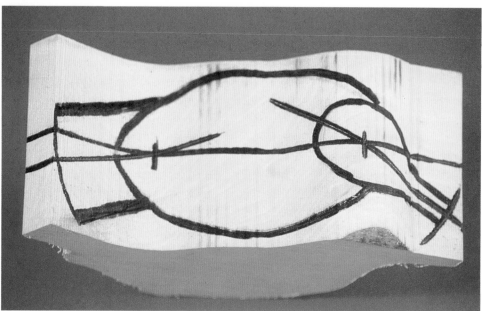

Fig 6.10 Marking out the blank using three centre-lines to turn the head and tail.

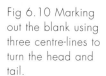

View the blank straight down the centre-line of the beak, tilting it back until you can only see along the head as far as the first pencilled line. Carve away the high portion that can be seen before tilting the head a little more, to reveal the next pencil line. Again, remove the visible high portion, and continue in this way until the back of the head is reached. Once this has been done, renew the pencil lines and repeat the process, this time working from the back of the head to the front. Some waste will also have to be removed from under the chin, so that the area where the neck meets the chest is at right angles to the centre-line of the head. If extra material was not left under the chin to cater for this, the throat may end up too far under the head.

If the series of pencil lines are now renewed, then viewing along the centre-line of the head should reveal them as a series of even parallel lines – quite different from the first time they were viewed – and the head shape should be nice and even, viewed from all angles. Turning the tail at an angle to the body presents less problems, but make sure that you allow sufficient extra thickness for the re-shaping.

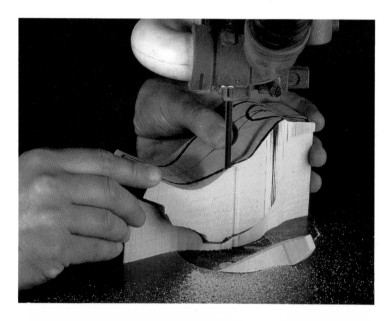

Fig 6.11 Using a cradle of scrap from the first cut to support the blank, whilst trimming off the rest of the waste.

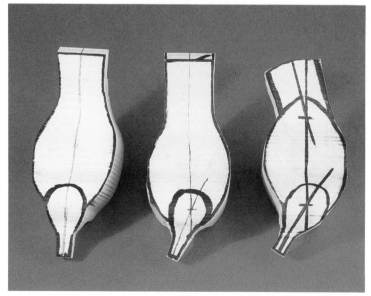

Fig 6.12 Compare the heads and tails of the three blanks.

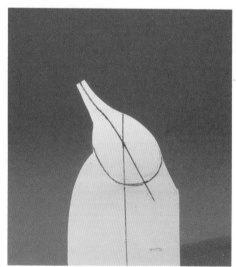

Fig 6.13 Turning the head along a different centre-line to the body creates some interesting problems.

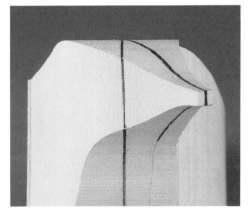

Fig 6.14 In this enlarged version, 'The Big Dipper', the head looks normal when viewed along the body centre-line . . .

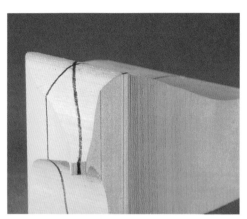

Fig 6.15 . . . However, when you look down the centre-line of the head, it looks oddly distorted . . .

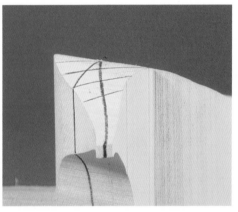

Fig 6.16 . . . Drawing lines at right angles to the head's centre-line shows up the problem even more!

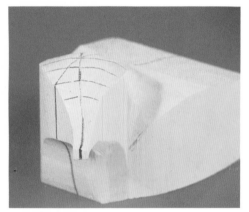

Fig 6.17 After correction, the parallel lines show that the head is evenly shaped.

Fig 6.18 Once the basic shape has been corrected, the head is ready for further work without fear of distortion.

CHAPTER 7

FEATHERS

There are two different types of feather to
be found in bird carving: the hard-edged
feathers which form the wings and tail, and
the soft-edged feathers which form the rest
of the body. The size and shape of hard-
edged feathers is fairly well defined, but the
soft-edged ones are less well defined and
often merge into an amorphous mass of
feathers that cover the rest of the body.

HARD-EDGED FEATHERS

These are well-defined in size and shape and
are suitable for carving in the form of small
steps in the surface of the carving. Many
beginners, however, try to cover the entire
bird with these sharply defined feathers and
end up with a result similar to a tiled roof —
this is to be avoided. They should normally
be confined to the wings, tail and crest of a
bird unless a windblown, ruffled-feather
look is required.

BASIC SHAPE
A common mistake with wing and tail
feathers it to make them far too flat, as if
they had been ironed. The cross section of
the feather is usually simplified for carving,
to a convex upper surface and a concave
lower one. By altering the curvature of the
lower surface in relation to the upper one,
making it slightly flatter, the feathers can be
considerably strengthened, as this will leave
a feather that is thin at the edge but thicker
in the middle. It is important to shape all
the feathers with a good curve on the upper
surface and, where they show, to make the
undersides concave, if realism is intended.

SURFACE RIPPLES
After the curved surface, the next thing that
you can do to a hard-edged feather to add to
the realism, is to carve in surface ripples.
These are put in as you form the basic shape

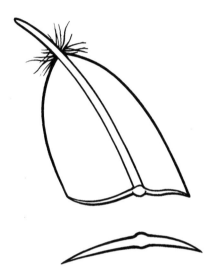

Fig 7.1 Typical cross section of flight feather,
simplified for carving to give additional
strength.

of the feather, because they will also make
the edge wavy. I add these to larger
feathers, where there is sufficient surface
area for the effect to show properly.

SPLITS AND BREAKS
Most beginners soon start to introduce a
few splits into feathers, usually using the
pyrograph when texturing. When you look
closely at how the feathers split, you will
see that they fall into three types, and that
when you get a split, the shape of the
feather edge changes too. It is useful to pick
up some wing and tail feathers and study the
shapes, cross sections and surface ripples,
and also to try the various feather splits and
see how they effect the feather edge
contours. The three forms of splits are: the
simple open split, the curl over the upper
surface, and the curl under the upper
surface, all of which really need to be
planned and drawn in before feather carving
commences, to get the maximum effect
from the changes in shape.

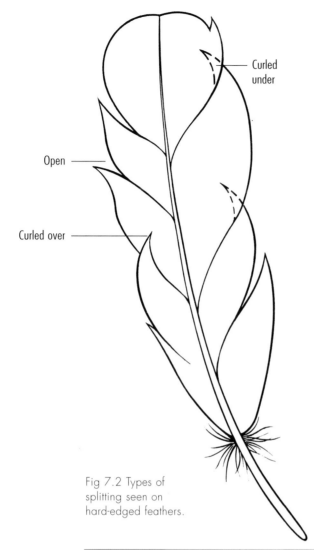

Curled
under

Open

Curled over

Fig 7.2 Types of
splitting seen on
hard-edged feathers.

CREATING HARD-EDGED FEATHERS

The first stage is to accurately and carefully draw the feathers onto the surface of the bird, complete with the planned splits. Care should be taken to get their size, shape and position as close as possible to the drawings. Because the carving is curved and the drawing flat, feathers take less space on the drawing and cannot just be traced. I plot the positions of the feather tips, drawing in lines where they occur, and I then spread the feathers out to fill the surface available on the carving. Unless the bird is very large, or the wings or tail are spread, no attempt is made to include every individual feather; each feather group showing is represented by a few feathers, the rest remaining stacked out of sight.

When all the feathers have been drawn onto the wings, identify the main feather groups, and carve a relief around the tips to form a step. This helps define the group, adds to the wing surface shape, and makes it easier to carve the feathers overlapping the group below them. A small sanding drum or smooth, cylindrical carbide or ruby burr can

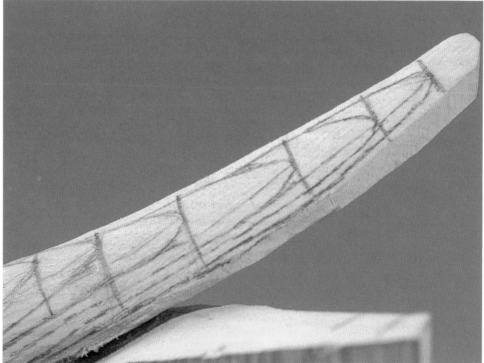

Fig 7.3 Marking the
wing tip positions
with a line allows
quick redrafting, to
get feather spacing
and spread correct.

be used. Where the pencil lines are carved away, they will need to be redrawn in readiness for the actual feather carving.

Most people outline the feathers with a stop cut, which is formed either with a knife or a pyrograph; an alternative is to outline the feather with a safe-ended cylindrical diamond cutter. If you use the cutter, you can change the shape of the feather as you go, without leaving stop cut marks cut into the feather surface. When using a stop cut, the feather edges can be relieved using a small skew chisel, knife, or cylindrical diamond burr. Ripples are also carved in at this stage, using various round abrasive stones – I use ones from ¼in (6mm), up to 1in (25mm) in diameter. Outline large quills using the safe-ended, diamond, cylindrical cutter before tidying up with the pyrograph burning pen, held at a shallow angle to the feather surface. To finish, sand them by hand, with very fine abrasive, to round them over. Small quills can be formed by simply holding the pyrograph pen at a shallow angle to the feather surface, and burning a line from each side of the quill, leaving it standing proud. Again, this is followed by fine sanding.

After completing the quills, I usually add a base texture of mini ripples with a small, fine abrasive, ball-shaped stone. I often then texture the hard-edged feathers with a small, inverted, cone-shaped, fine white abrasive stone, before finally texturing them using a well-honed pyrograph tip, run at a medium heat so that the lines can be set very close to each other. It is important to

Avoid Christmas tree effect of straight lines

Curved feather barbs are softer and more natural

Colouring and shading can be added

Fig 7.5 Texture lines created with the pyrograph.

keep them close, and to thoroughly cover the entire feather surface. The burn lines should be curved and started right up against the quill, so that the lines cover any areas left bare by the texturing stones.

Again, this is a simplification of the shape, adopted for ease of burning in one pass – the barbs are more often seen as a soft S shape. Variation in the burnt texture can be achieved by starting the burn line slowly, speeding up along the line, and flicking off at the end. This gives a deeper, darker burn at the quill and a lighter, shallower burn at the edge. By burning both from the edge of the feather, and from the quill towards the centre of each side, you can burn the soft S shape more easily. It is important not to nick the shaft with the stone or pyrograph, as this shows when painted and is very difficult to disguise.

Hold the pyrograph at a shallow angle to the surface

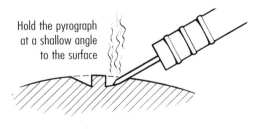

After sanding

Fig 7.4 Burning the quill.

The pyrograph can be used to undercut the edges of some feathers, to give more separation between overlapping feathers, and one or two deeper, heavier burn lines can be added to simulate small splits, which don't alter the edge contour. It can also be used to get some separation of feather tips, which is difficult to achieve with ordinary tools; the pyrograph is a very useful carving tool for adding fine details and tidying up awkward corners.

CREATING SOFT-EDGED FEATHERS

With the hard-edged feathers complete the soft feather areas, which invariably overlap the hard feathers, are carved and textured. There are two ways to tackle these: either carve them as individual feathers (individually carved and raised first, or left flat), or represent them by an overall texture. An overall texture is often chosen by carvers as it is quicker to do, and done well, can be just as effective as carving individual feathers. In fact, in some soft feather areas, individual feathers are so indistinct they can only be easily created by a texture. Textures made with a stone tend to look softer, while texturing with the pyrograph is harder and more hairlike, so it is possible to vary the type of texture to suit the feather and subject.

CREATING A MUSCLED APPEARANCE

I usually carve the surface into clumps of feathers first, to break up the smooth regular body surface. My carvings have a characteristic lumpy, muscled look, created by the use of a fairly heavy under-texture of feather groups. These feather groups and lumps are also used to imply underlying body form. I carve them quite deeply into the surface before softening their edges to blend smoothly into adjacent areas. Breaking up the surface of the carving in this way helps to make the finished feather effect look

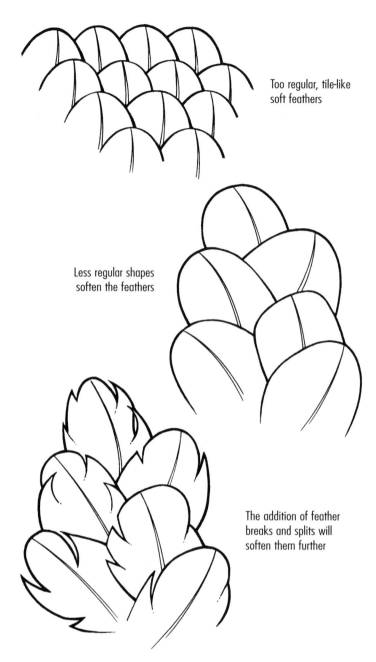

Too regular, tile-like soft feathers

Less regular shapes soften the feathers

The addition of feather breaks and splits will soften them further

Fig 7.6 Creating soft-edged feathers.

softer, as it takes away the regular, hard outline of the overall shape. Once this is done, the surface can have individual feathers carved over it, or just be textured.

Texturing should always be built up as a series of layers, starting with the coarsest and working through to the finest. Different sizes and shapes of abrasive stone give different types of texture line, and the finest, hair-like lines are created with the pyrograph.

The base texture is a series of gently curved lines, usually formed with a stone that gives broader, coarser marks. The lines follow the flow lines over the body, but are relatively random, and do not cover the whole surface; this adds shape and flow to the finished texture. It is also possible to carve a hint of individual feathers as an alternative base texture. These are carved by using a round stone to lightly outline the individual feathers, and will show through a flow-line texture to give the impression of individual feathers.

After the base texture, a second layer should be carved using a stone that gives a medium-weight mark, to cover more of the surface with short, curved strokes, still following the flow lines of the body. I then give a final texture using a small, cylindrical, fine white stone, working over the base textures. For this layer I cover the entire surface with short, overlapping curved lines, leaving no untextured timber. If a fine hair-like, feather effect is required, the final texturing should be done with a pyrograph.

To make sure that the texturing overlaps in the same way that the feathers do, start texturing from the back and work forward. This also makes sure that the whole surface is completely textured, with no gaps or thin spots.

An alternative to texturing the soft feather areas like this, is to draw individual feathers over the previously carved, lumpy feather groups, and to texture these as a series of overlapping, but loosely defined, individual feathers. More complex still, is to carve and shape each of these feathers into a soft mound, before texturing them individually. The shapes of soft-edged feathers are not as rigidly maintained as hard-edged ones, so a deliberate attempt must be made when drawing them on, to get variation in their shapes, to prevent the effect becoming too regular.

Texturing is the one area where the techniques of carvers vary, and one where experimentation and practise pays real dividends. Texture some samples with the various tools at your disposal to find out what marks they make on the timber, and then try them in different combinations to see what effects you can achieve: remember always to texture in short, curved strokes and not straight lines. I shape each individual feather surface like a convex shell, but I don't outline the edges of these soft feathers with a stop cut, as they should 'melt' into each other without a clearly defined edge.

The slightly exaggerated, puffed up look given to each feather will give a soft appearance to the finished carving. When all the soft feathers have been relieved and shaped, sand them before further texturing. I sand each feather carefully so that the individual feather shape is retained. A very smooth finish is required before texturing and some carvers dampen the wood slightly with alcohol or warm water to raise the grain before a final sanding with 400 or 600 grit paper, but I usually finish off with a Scotchbrite pad mounted on an arbor, which leaves a silky smooth surface.

I like to texture individual soft feathers with a stone, sometimes in combination with a pyrograph. It is worth spending time experimenting with different combinations of stones and burning, as the final results can vary considerably. Make up some small sample pieces and try out the different combinations of carving and texturing methods for soft feathers, then seal and paint them white. You will then be able to see how the different combinations effect the look of the finished feathers, to help choose the right combination for the effect you want to achieve.

The completed effect should resemble soft, feather-like shapes flowing into each other in all directions, without a trace of a hard line surrounding the feathers, and only an almost indistinguishable transition from one to the next. Again, it is a good idea to study real body feathers; as I have said before, the part you usually see is like the iceberg, only the tip. Try holding a shell-shaped, soft feather against a hard surface, convex side uppermost, and push it around to see how much the shape can change. When going for realism, you cannot have too much knowledge of your subject – good research is always the key to bringing out the best in your work.

CHAPTER 8

LEGS

There is a wide variation in the development of birds' feet and toes. Most birds' feet have four toes, three facing forward and one, the hallux, attached to the inside of the leg and pointing backwards, but this arrangement of toes does vary in different species. Woodpeckers, for example, mainly have two toes facing forwards and two facing back, and the hallux has been lost on some birds, or is raised part way up the leg like the pads on a dog. It can be seen then, that feet and legs need to be as closely observed as the rest of a bird when gathering information.

Feet and legs are almost always needed when creating a realistic carving; very few poses hide them completely, although you may get away with just a couple of toes peeping out from under the feathers.

There is a fairly comprehensive range of American-made, cast pewter legs and feet available in Britain, and fortunately, the legs and feet made for the American birds are often a reasonable match, both in terms of actual dimensions, and of bulk or weight, for various UK species. If not, they can often be adapted quite successfully. Legs and feet may even be made from scratch.

MODIFYING CAST LEGS

Where a suitable complete leg and foot is not available, the easiest option is to try finding a suitable foot: small songbird feet may also be suitable for use in carving miniatures of much larger birds. You can then cut off the leg and drill the foot to take a brass or steel wire, and flesh this out with moulded epoxy putty to form the leg. This is the same technique as used to create a full foot and leg, but is much quicker, because

the most difficult bit of the modelling is avoided. Sometimes, with a sitting pose, the leg is not even required and the foot alone will do anyway.

Even if a cast leg and foot of suitable size is available, it may not be appropriate to utilize it, because the pegs that locate it in the base and the body only give a very restricted range of possible alignments. You might want to fix the legs at a rather different angle to the body and base than the cast fixing pegs allow, or perhaps depict one leg drawn up towards the body in a resting pose or a low crouching position, or one foot grasping a near vertical surface.

The cast metal legs are fairly strong, but they are brittle and can only be bent slightly without danger of them snapping, even if, as often recommended, they are heated with a hairdryer first. Besides this, they tend not to bend at the joints because these are thicker than the sections between them so they bow or buckle when attempts are made to modify them. Larger legs are reinforced with steel piano wire, and cannot really be bent at all. Toes, because they are so thin and fragile, need to be bent by cutting small notches in the underside, or they will crack and break off.

Bird legs are generally one of four main types, so be careful to mould the leg in the correct style for the species you are carving. The four main types are:

1 Feather-covered, which you would usually carve in wood rather than model, making only the toes and claws.

2 Smooth legs, with no apparent scales.

3 Legs with definite, overlapping scales.

4 Reticulated or plated legs, covered in a pattern of many small plates.

FITTING A NEW LEG TO A COMMERCIAL FOOT

1 Cut off the leg and the peg beneath the foot. I use electricians' endcutters, but a fine saw would work just as well.

2 Clean up the casting where you have removed the parts, to give a flat surface to accurately drill from.

3 Using a pointed awl, mark a centre for the hole you are going to drill.

4 Using a hand-held drill, drill through the foot at the correct angle for the new leg/foot peg. I use my flexi-shaft, and keep $\frac{1}{8}$ and $\frac{3}{32}$ in (3 and 2.5mm) diameter drills for jobs like this. Support the foot on a block of wood whilst drilling, and wear a leather glove to protect your holding hand from the drill and the heat!

5 Bend a brass or steel wire, smaller in diameter than the finished leg, into the correct form of the foot peg, leg, and body peg. Try them on your carving at this stage, because these legs cannot be satisfactorily modified later. The hole in the foot can be opened up with a round needle file if necessary, to allow it to sit correctly.

6 Hold the foot and leg in the correct positions; I use a small modellers' 'third hand' clamp and a block of Plasticine for this, pressing the foot into the Plasticine to hold it firmly on the table, and holding the leg wire in place with the clamp.

7 Apply superglue sparingly, and sprinkle on some baking powder; this makes the glue set immediately, and gives it good gap-filling properties. I find this is better than using the thickened superglues, and the process can be repeated if necessary.

8 Clean up the foot to leg wire joint, and roughen the leg wire with sandpaper, or, if the leg is to be thick, use the superglue and baking powder to give a good bonding surface for the epoxy putty.

9 Mix up some epoxy ribbon putty, first removing the centre strip where the two colours meet, which can be granular. Kneading a piece of Plasticine first will prevent the epoxy sticking to your fingers.

10 Draw out the putty into a flat, narrow ribbon (it is this property that makes the ribbon epoxy most suitable for the job), and wind this around the leg wire, in a thin covering.

11 Apply a little more putty where the joints are, and put a thin sausage of putty down the back of the leg, to give the typical oval section.

12 Gently mould the putty with your fingers, to smooth and shape it.

13 Create creases, scales and pad textures in the putty surface with dental tools and blunted hypodermic needles. Use one of the original cast feet as reference, and keep pushing the tools into a block of Plasticine as you work, to stop the tools sticking. Make sure that the leg is given the correct texture for the species you are carving (*see* page 56).

14 When you are happy with the shape and modelling, put the leg aside to dry. Once the epoxy putty has set, it can be further carved, if required, using cross cut rotary burrs or needle files.

15 Fit the legs to the carving using epoxy adhesive.

16 When the glue has cured, place a small ring of epoxy ribbon putty around the top of the leg, and use it to blend the leg tuft to the leg.

17 Texture and draw out the ribbon putty into the surrounding textured areas with a pointed dental tool or wire.

Fig 8.1 Using superglue and baking powder to attach the drilled, cast foot to the new leg wire. If the wire is thick it should be bent to shape first.

Fig 8.2 Ribbon epoxy putty is mixed to model the leg. The central section where the two colours meet, which is part set and granular, is discarded.

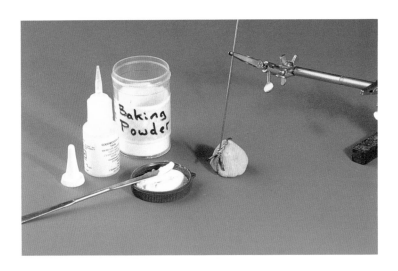

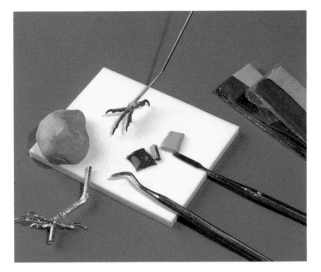

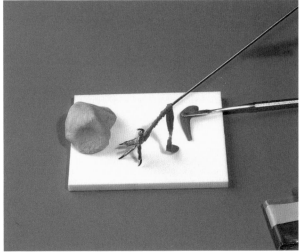

Fig 8.3 When mixed, ribbon epoxy putty is highly ductile and can be drawn out into a thin ribbon, and wrapped around the leg wire.

Fig 8.4 The epoxy is moulded to shape with fingers and dental tools; scales and marks can be impressed after the leg is shaped, or carved with burrs when it is set.

MAKING LEGS FROM SCRATCH

This technique is very similar to that used for fitting a new leg to a foot except that you will have to make a complete metal skeleton for the leg. If you take dimensions from a taxidermy specimen, the leg will probably be shrivelled enough for you to copy it in metal and then cover it thinly with epoxy. The thinner you can keep the epoxy covering, the less likely the leg is to look lumpy, uneven and homemade. I make the basic leg skeleton from brass wire, which can be bought in a wide range of sizes from most model shops, then cover it in epoxy putty. Small feet are rather fiddly to produce like this though, and for smaller birds, there is usually a cast foot available that is suitable for use in the previous method. Small legs can be produced from scratch with care and patience, although you may not be able to drill the toes for the leg wire, making soldering up more difficult unless you make a loop with the wire, to form an eye on the end for location.

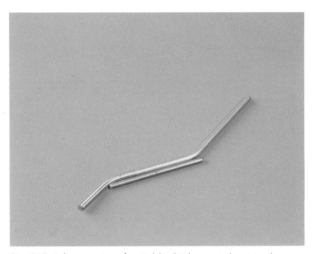

Fig 8.5 A brass wire of suitable thickness is bent to the correct angles to form the leg and mounting pins, and a second piece of wire is cut to make the leg shape more oval in cross section.

Fig 8.6 Annealed brass wire is bent and hammered on a steel block to get the section suitable for shaping the claw.

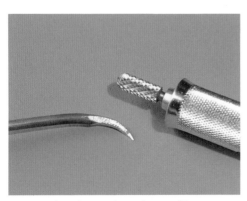

Fig 8.7 The claw is shaped using files or cross cut, rotary burrs.

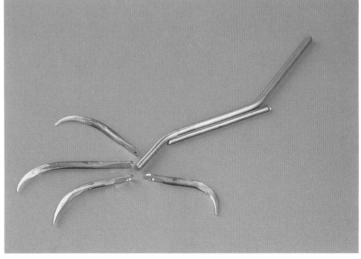

Fig 8.8 The leg and finished toes ready for assembly. Very thin wire toes can have an eye formed on the end, using roundnose pliers, instead of being drilled.

Fig 8.9 All the sections are wired together with florists' wire, on a temporary wooden support. Getting the correct position is much easier when the toes can actually be slipped onto the leg.

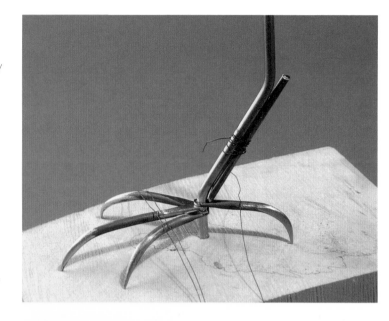

Fig 8.10 All parts are soldered with soft, electrical-grade solder and plumbers' flux.

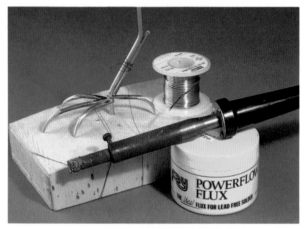

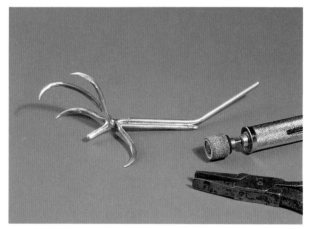

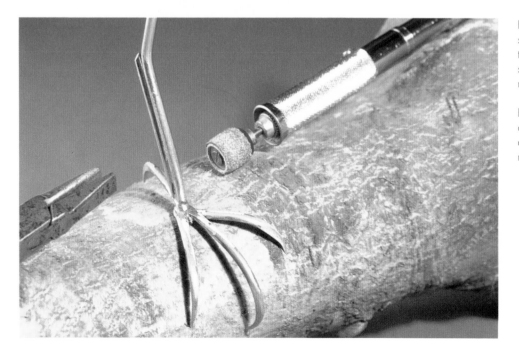

Fig 8.11 After soldering, the joint is trimmed, and excess solder and metal are removed.

Fig 8.12 The toes are given a final adjustment to suit the mounting.

Fig 8.13 Ribbon epoxy putty is wrapped around the toes and then the leg, then moulded and modelled to achieve the desired result.

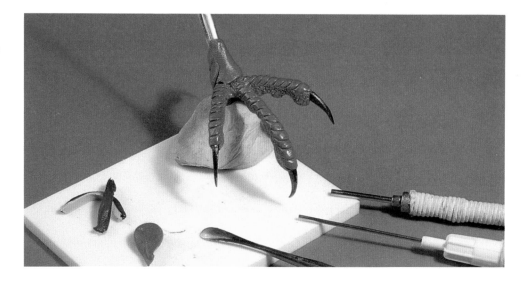

Fig 8.14 When the modelling is finished, the leg is set aside for 24 hours to dry.

Fig 8.15 A completed peregrine falcon leg after painting, ready for fitting to the carving.

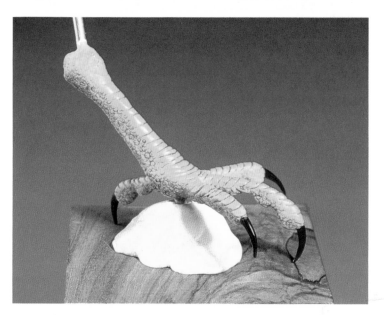

MODELLING A COMPLETE LEG AND FOOT

1 Measure and bend the main leg wire, forming a peg that will extend below the foot to fit into the base, and a peg that extends above the leg to fit into the body.

2 If the leg is large, cut a second, slightly smaller diameter wire to fit down the back of the leg so that in cross section, it forms a figure 8.

3 Take a long length of brass wire of the correct diameter for the toes, and anneal to soften the last ½in (13mm) by heating it to cherry red and then quenching it in water. Bend and flatten the end with a hammer, on a steel block, to form the approximate shape of the claw. The metal may have to be resoftened whilst working, especially when working with thicker wire, or it may crack.

4 Bend the toe and file to shape with needle files; shaping can also be done with a cross cut burr or small, rigid sanding drum used in a flexi-shaft.

5 Cut the toe off over-length, and soften the other end.

6 Flatten this end at right angles to the claw, so that a hole can be drilled to take the leg wire, making final assembly and soldering easier. Once the wire has been flattened enough, drill the correct size hole, then file down the thickness of the wire at this hole so that the four toes will sit nearly together, without one sitting higher than the others, and without too great a thickness of metal at the base of the leg.

7 When all four toes have been made, clean all the parts with abrasive paper, and assemble them on a wooden block, using nails and florists' iron binding wire to keep the parts in position. Keep the wire away from the actual joints, so that it doesn't get soldered in.

8 Soft solder all the joints using electricians' flux-cored solder and a heavy-duty soldering iron. In addition to this, I use some plumbers' flux brushed onto the joints. A small gas blowtorch could also be used, with care.

9 When cool, remove the binding wire and wash off the flux in hot water. Try the leg on the carving, and adjust it to sit comfortably on the base, as it cannot be adjusted once the putty has been put on. Needle files, cross cut rotary cutters or a sanding drum can then be used to clean up the leg prior to covering it with epoxy putty.

10 Start by covering the toes – if the foot is large, only work on a couple of toes at a time. When all the toes have been wrapped in putty, add extra balls of putty to form the pads, and then smooth and mould them with your fingers and a polished metal tool. I use a dental technicians' wax modelling tool.

11 Check the foot against the base to make sure the pads will sit correctly against it. Form scales with a polished metal dental tool, and texture the pads with small metal tubes (blunt hypodermic needles or the needles from computer printer inkjet refills) to give a rough, knobbly texture, or a pointed tool to give a fine texture.

12 When the toes have hardened up enough to handle, wrap the leg with putty, and form any webbed areas between the toes. Texture the leg and webs in a similar manner to the toes.

13 When the modelling is finished, it should be set aside for 24 hours to dry. The legs and feet can then be further refined, if necessary, by carving and sanding, before fitting them to the carved bird.

CHAPTER 9

EYES

The eyes are the focal point of the head just as the head is the focal point of the bird, and the success of the head depends on how well those eyes are positioned, set and finished. They are a feature that give problems to many carvers, and the only real 'secret of success' is to keep practising: eyes can be fitted and removed quite easily, as can eye rings, so if they don't look right the first time, just have another try!

TYPES OF EYE

Glass eyes are available in several styles and qualities; the cheapest are the black glass beads on wire. As most of the iris gets hidden by the eye ring on small birds' eyes (under $\frac{1}{4}$in (6mm)), unless the iris is a bright colour like white, red or yellow, I fit black bead eyes, carefully selecting a matching pair because they vary considerably in size and shape.

Flat-backed eyes on wire are the next cheapest to buy, and are available in all the sizes and pupil colours that are needed for birds. They have a clear glass front portion, with the iris colour on the back. Unfortunately this means that, viewed from certain angles, the eye can appear as plain glass, so I only use this type on stylized work.

The best quality glass eyes are the aspheric, or convex/concave eyes which have a curved rather than a flat back, so that the coloured iris is also curved and covered by a more even layer of clear glass. These look far better when viewed from all angles, but are, of course, the most expensive. However, the cost of the eyes compared with the time taken in the carving is extremely small, and the extra cost of the better eyes is easily justified. Multi-coloured irises are also available for that extra special project; the eye supplier will advise what eyes are suitable for your project if you are in doubt.

You can buy eyes, with a clear glass iris and black pupil, and paint them yourself. They seem to be an attractive idea, and I have had the best results painting them with modellers' enamel paints used on the plastic kits, or filling them with coloured epoxy glue. In the long term, however, I have found that the paint and the epoxy film sometimes parts company with the glass, and the resulting minute air space gives a mirror effect akin to some sun glasses! This is probably caused by the differing rates of movement of the glass, epoxy, wood and paint – eyes painted with acrylic paint exhibit the phenomenon very quickly, often after a matter of only a few weeks.

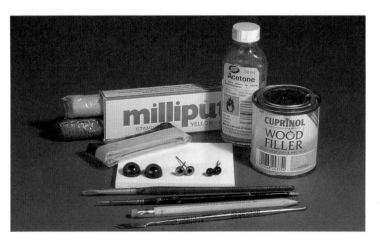

Fig 9.1 The three common types of glass eye (left: convex/concave; centre: coloured, flat-backed on wire; right: black glass bead on wire), with the tools and materials to set them and form eyelids.

SETTING THE EYE

First check that the eye positions are going to match each side of the head – you don't want your carving to be christened Isaiah! If one side is a little off, open up the hole in the worst side to allow the eye to be floated to the correct position on the putty. If the positions look alright, then before the head is sanded for texturing, the eyes should be tried in their sockets to make sure they are not too tight a fit. Some free movement is necessary, so that they can be positioned correctly. The corners of the eye

hole can then be rounded over and softened by sanding with a piece of rolled-up abrasive. The eye sockets are now ready and texturing can be done right up to the edge of the eye hole.

I fit the eyes on a bed of epoxy putty, but some carvers use plastic wood, or even Plasticine. I don't favour the latter as the oil from the modelling clay seeps into the timber and may affect the painting in the long term. I use the stick-type putty, which is displaced around the eye as it is pushed into the head and positioned. I press the eye in and adjust it with the eraser end of a

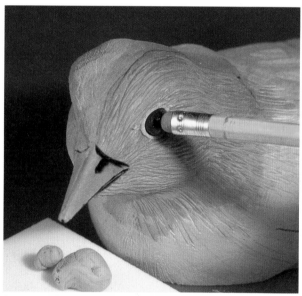

Fig 9.2 Fill the eye cavity with epoxy putty.

Fig 9.3 Insert the eye, positioning it with the eraser end of a pencil.

Fig 9.4 Removing the excess putty displaced by the eye.

pencil; this doesn't slip and won't scratch the glass, and it also allows pressure to be applied off-centre, making the eye tilt in the socket to get the correct position. I then scrape away the excess putty which is forced out around the eye, so that the eye is unobscured and the final positioning can be checked. The putty can be scraped away with virtually anything that is to hand – I use an old dental tool.

Both flat-backed and convex/concave eyes should be fitted with the back of the eye perpendicular to the vertical axis of the head, but tilted inwards towards the front, making the bird look forward. The eyes should not look startled or like organ stops – if the eye won't push in deep enough and position correctly, the hole is too small, and will need cleaning out and enlarging. Viewed from the back of the head the eyes should be obscured, from the top they may be just visible, and when viewed directly from the front, they should stare back at you.

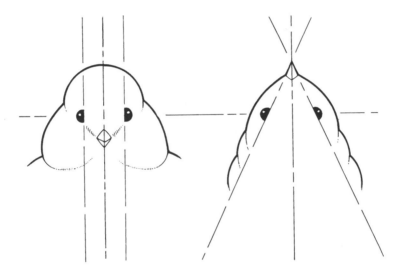

Fig 9.5 Alignment of flat-backed glass eyes.

Fig 9.6 The eye correctly set and cleaned up, ready to form the eyelid.

EYE RINGS

I make the eyelid, or eye ring, from a small roll of epoxy ribbon putty, which is more ductile than the variety I use to set the eyes. When mixing epoxy ribbon putty, always remove a centre strip where the two colours touch, as it is usually gritty. I roll it out with my fingertips, on a small piece of acrylic plastic. Rubbing a lump of Plasticine over the plastic and kneading a piece in your fingers will prevent the putty sticking to you or the plastic. The Plasticine leaves a minute trace of oil on everything, so when you cut a section off the roll to put around the eye, push the knife into a piece of Plasticine first. Arrange the roll of epoxy putty around the eye, and fix it by

carefully using a pointed dental tool to squash and draw the putty from the outer edge of the ring into the texturing. If it is fixed in one or two places first, minor adjustments can be made to the shape of the eye ring before finishing it. Look at reference photographs to determine how the eye ring looks; it may appear perfectly round or have distinct corners depending on the mood of the bird. The finished eye ring can be textured using a small metal tube; I use an assortment of different sized hypodermic needles with the points stoned flat, to give a knobbly look to the eye ring. Ribbon epoxy can also be used to form a partly closed eye, by bringing the epoxy down over the surface of the eye to form the eye lid.

Fig 9.7 After mixing, the putty is rolled out into a thin round strip and cut to length, to fit round the eye.

Fig 9.8 The strip is placed around the eye and fixed in position by drawing the putty out into the texturing.

Fig 9.9 The eye ring is textured using a small metal tube – I keep several blunted hypodermic needles for the job.

Fig 9.10 The finished eye with textured eye ring.

An alternative method, which many beginners find easier, is to build up a small fillet of plastic wood around and onto the eye. Using a small brush and lots of thinners, the filler is smoothed out and the eye opening shaped. It is important to use the type of plastic wood filler that is marked inflammable, as the newer, water-based types will raise the grain. The thinner for most of the plastic woods is acetone, and a small bottle can be obtained from chemists. When the filler is skinned over, but not fully dried, use a small, blunt, dental tool to press down the filler around the eye, to form an eye ring. When the plastic wood is fully dried, it can be carefully carved or burnished with the pyrograph, on a very low heat setting, to improve the eye ring shape.

If you should scratch an eye, they are a fairly soft, lead crystal type of glass, you can either replace it, or varnish it to hide the scratch. Carefully applied clear nail polish will do the trick, or you could try acrylic gloss medium.

Fig 9.11 A fillet of plastic wood is built up around the eye; avoid using too much filler.

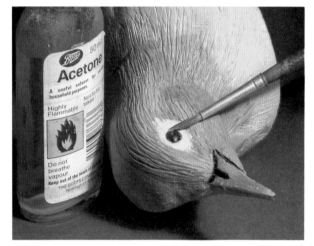

Fig 9.12 A brush and thinners are used to smooth out and shape the eye area.

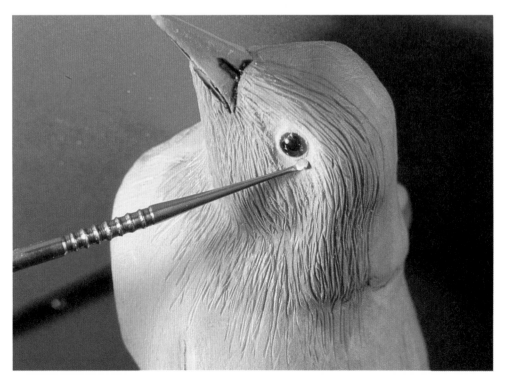

Fig 9.13 When the plastic wood has a dry skin on the surface, the area around the eye is gently depressed with a metal tool, to form an eye ring. When fully dry, this can be further textured by carving, or burning with the pyrograph set at a low heat.

CHAPTER 10

PAINTING

This chapter covers the area that holds most fears for carvers, who often do not consider themselves to be artists. However, one of the most difficult things to create on a flat surface is a three-dimensional effect, and you have already created most of this by carving, so that is one hurdle already passed!

Basic painting techniques are not difficult to master, though they do require practise and it is no good waiting until you have carved that masterpiece to start playing with paints. You need to develop your painting skills alongside those required for the carving, so start experimenting with paint mixes and brush techniques early, to keep your painting skills up. You can buy American castings of carved birds and paint them over and over – good ones also provide valuable reference information on carving procedures. You could also practise many of the techniques by painting on plain white card, carved wooden practise pieces, or even your rejects!

PAINTS

The two types of paint generally used by bird carvers are oils and acrylics. Oils are a traditional medium, and are considered by some to be better for blending than acrylics and to give a superior finish, but their working properties, especially their slowness of drying, mean that more painting skills and patience are required than for working in acrylic.

Acrylics are modern, plastic, emulsion-based paints, which are now favoured by the majority of bird artists in the UK and the USA, for their ease and speed of use. Although acrylics can be thinned with water, once dry, they are water-resistant, flexible and durable – and acrylic mediums do not yellow with age like oils. Most of the pigments used are extremely lightfast, and they are available in a vast range of pre-mixed colours and shades. Colour can be built up layer by layer, speeding up the process by using warm air from a hairdryer, so that it is touch dry and ready for the next coat in minutes.

Basic acrylic wash painting techniques are quickly learnt by complete novices, and then it is just a matter of practise to build up levels of skill. For these reasons, I will only deal here with acrylic paints and the techniques of using them.

Various makes of artist quality acrylic paints are available, and these can be freely mixed without adverse effects. They vary in consistency from brand to brand and range to range, depending upon the ratio of pigment to acrylic medium. I prefer the 'flow' mixes which can be brushed straight from the tube; they are easier to mix evenly, and I can use them neat on stylized carvings. One range that is particularly liked by bird carvers is an acrylic gouache mix, the Jo Sonja range from Chroma Acrylics. These have slightly different working properties, but impart a lovely velvet, almost matt finish, to which you can add your own glossier sheen where required. Conventional acrylics tend to become glossier as the paint film gets thicker, and once there, the sheen cannot be removed.

Acrylic gesso is used as an undercoat on birds to promote good adhesion, and in my style of painting it is usually tinted to the lightest base colour on the bird. It is often used in place of Titanium White, in acrylic paint mixes. It has very good adhesion to the carving surface, and contains a powdered filler which gives a good matt base for the acrylic wash painting technique.

COLOUR

Colours of paints vary from one manu-facturer to another, even if the colour has the same name; Jo Sonja Payne's Gray is much bluer than the Rowney Cryla Flow equivalent, as can be seen in the sample paint mixes. This means that you cannot follow paint mixes in a book, unless you are using exactly the same brand as they used. Except where I have noted otherwise, the mixes in this book use Jo Sonja acrylic gouache paints. The one colour that I don't use from the Jo Sonja range is Ultramarine, as I think the mixes made with it look milky – I always use the Rowney Cryla Flow Ultramarine. Collecting the different manufacturers' colour charts will enable you to make informed comparisons between colours. Turner's Yellow for instance, is a slightly lighter shade of Yellow Oxide or Yellow Ochre in other paint ranges, and is probably equivalent to Golden Ochre in the Jo Sonja range. Colour mixes using such equivalents, however, may still not be totally successful.

PAINT MIXING CHARTS

Beginners often look for a magic paint mixing chart – they really don't exist. Some suppliers offer mixing wheels and swatches, but they are of little use for bird painting, as they offer only a small range of the colours and shades needed for birds, amongst loads of colours you will never want. The solution is to produce your own charts, learning about colour mixing as you go. The first thing to do when you get some paints is to experiment, to find out what the basic colours look like and how they mix, and it is while you are doing this that you can create your own paint mixing charts, covering the colours you will need later.

Get some smooth, white, A4 card from your printers or stationers, and lightly pencil in some $^3/_4$in squares to take the sample colours, leaving room to write the mix underneath. Start by making a colour chart of your basic colours – because of the constraints of the printing process, the printed card from the art shop bears only a passing resemblance to the actual colours from the tube. Thin some of the paint with water to make a thin wash and paint a square on the card, then overpaint half the square with neat colour. You can now see how the colour looks both as a wash and as solid colour; you could also include a heavier wash to show the intermediate stage. The wash will indicate whether the base colour of a brown, for instance, is red or yellow, and will give a better idea of how a wash of that colour is likely to influence any colour beneath it.

After creating a basic colour chart, start to try various colour mixes. The idea is to make colour mix charts that will be useful

Fig 10.1 A manufacturer's paint colour chart and some of my home-made, colour mixing reference charts.

in the future, so variations on blacks and whites are a good place to start. I use a double column of squares to make up my colour charts, with the first column for the paint, and the second to note the colours used, and how many parts of each. Carbon Black and Titanium White are not colours that would normally be put straight onto a bird, except possibly as a highlight. If you look closely at a black area on a bird, you will see that the black is either warm, with a hint of brown, cool, with a hint of blue, or perhaps greenish, or still another colour. Whites also tend to fall into warm (brown) or cool (blue), and very occasionally neutral (gray) tones. Interest and realism in the painting of individual feathers is aided greatly by using two or three distinct shades of the same colour to paint what, at first, might appear to be a single shade. Usually, a feather is given a darker base and lighter edges over the basic colour, but don't mix warm and cool versions of the same colour

together. It is important that the tones are different enough to be distinguished from each other at a normal viewing distance, not just with the carving a few inches from your nose while you paint it!

Mixes are very difficult to gauge exactly and are only an indication of how a colour was achieved; trying to recreate mixes using percentages is just about impossible. In this book I have given mixes in terms of equal parts. I usually use the amount I can pick up on the tip of a small palette knife, about the size of a small pea, as one part. It doesn't really matter what you use, just try to keep it consistent, and expect to make minor corrections as you go.

PAINT MIXES
Try some of the following mixes in various ratios: they will provide a start to a range of colours which you will find useful when painting birds. Don't forget to make samples of both a wash and full colour.

WARM WHITES

BASIC MIX Mix 1 part Raw Umber with various ratios of white gesso, from 1 to 20 parts. (I use Liquitex gesso and use it instead of white most of the time.)

VARIATIONS These colours can be warmed by the addition of a very small amount of Yellow Oxide to the mix.

ALTERNATIVE Repeat, using from 1 to 20 parts Liquitex Raw Umber and see the difference between brands!

MIX A

MIX B

MIX C

MIX D

MIX E

MIX F

MIX G

COOL WHITES

BASIC MIX Mix 1 part Payne's Gray with from 1 to 40 parts of white gesso.

VARIATIONS The addition of a little black will make the mixes more neutral.

MIX A   **MIX B**   **MIX C**

MIX D   **MIX E**   **MIX F**   **MIX G**

ALTERNATIVE Repeat, using Rowney Cryla Flow Payne's Gray to get a totally different, but equally useful range of colours.

MIX A   **MIX B**   **MIX C**

MIX D   **MIX E**   **MIX F**   **MIX G**

Fig 10.2 My basic kit for paint mixing and brush cleaning.

VARIATIONS ON WHITES

MIX A
Warm White

MIX B
1 part Warm
White to 1 part
Smoked Pearl

MIX C
1 part Warm
White to 1 part
Nimbus Gray

MIX D
4 parts Warm
White to 2 parts
Smoked Pearl to 1
part Nimbus Gray

MIX E
Mix D plus 1 part
Nimbus Gray

MIX F
2 parts Warm
White to 1 part
Smoked Pearl

MIX G
4 parts Titanium
White to 1 part
Nimbus Gray

MIXING TIP These mixes will probably
have given you as wide a range of whites,
grays, blue grays and beiges as you could
possibly wish, but you could add a range
of neutral grays by mixing 1 part Liquitex
Neutral Gray, value 5, to various ratios of
white gesso. Liquitex make several
different values of neutral gray!

Fig 10.3 The basic
equipment: brushes,
paints, and
mediums.

BLACKS AND BROWNS

BASIC MIX Mix 1 part Ultramarine Blue (Rowney Cryla Flow) with from 1 to 12 parts Burnt Sienna.

VARIATIONS Try mixing 1 part Carbon Black with 1, 2 and 4 parts of the following: Pine Green, Pthalo Green, Pthalo Blue, Ultramarine Blue, Diox Purple, and Burnt Umber.

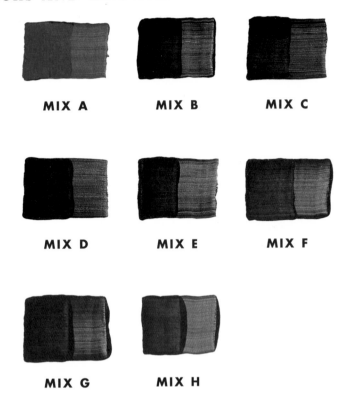

MIX A **MIX B** **MIX C**

MIX D **MIX E** **MIX F**

MIX G **MIX H**

ALTERNATIVE Repeat, adding Burnt Umber to the Ultramarine instead. With only these two colour mixes you can create an amazing range of browns and blacks; it will quickly become one of your most useful mixes.

MIXING TIP Small quantities of the correct hue of pearlescent powder can be added to the mixes to give a hint of iridescence – don't overdo it though!

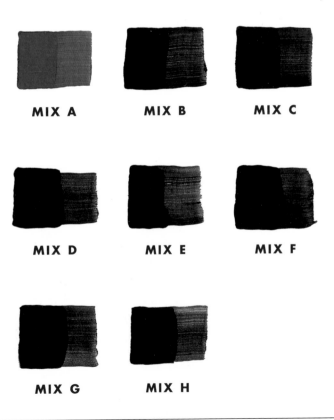

MIX A **MIX B** **MIX C**

MIX D **MIX E** **MIX F**

MIX G **MIX H**

VARIATIONS ON ORANGE BROWNS

MIX A
1 part Burnt Sienna to 1 part Burnt Umber

MIX B
2 parts Burnt Sienna to 2 parts Burnt Umber to 1 part Ultramarine Blue

MIX C
1 part Burnt Sienna to 1 part Burnt Umber to 1 part Ultramarine Blue

MIX D
1 part Burnt Umber to 2 parts Burnt Sienna

MIX E
1 part Burnt Umber to 1 part Burnt Sienna to 1 part Raw Sienna

MIX F
1 part Burnt Umber to 1 part Burnt Sienna to 2 parts Raw Sienna

VARIATIONS ON STRAW

MIX A
1 part gesso to 1 part Raw Sienna

MIX B
1 part gesso to 1 part Yellow Oxide to 1 part Raw Sienna

MIX C
2 parts gesso to 1 part Yellow Oxide to 1 part Raw Sienna

MIX D
1 part Burnt Sienna to 1 part gesso to 1 part Yellow Oxide

MIX E
1 part Burnt Sienna to 1 part Yellow Oxide to 1 part Norwegian Orange

MIX F
2 parts Burnt Sienna to 1 part Yellow Oxide to 1 part Norwegian Orange

For pale straw colours and orange browns, try mixes of Raw Sienna and Gesso, or Burnt Sienna and Gesso, adding Yellow Oxide for a more yellow hue, or Norwegian Orange for a more orange hue.

You can keep your finished cards in a binder or filing box for instant reference, and whenever you try to create a new colour, keep a permanent record the same way. Soon paint mixing will become much easier, through a combination of experience and your newly created, personal, colour mixing reference cards.

BASIC RANGE OF PAINTS AND MEDIUMS

Below, I have listed the basic painting materials for the dipper; additional items can be acquired as needed, and I have also listed those which I would buy first. Although initially expensive, some colours are used in very small amounts, so replacements are gradual and their cost will be spread.

PAINTS USED ON THE DIPPER

- White Gesso (Liquitex)
- Raw Umber
- Raw Sienna
- Burnt Sienna
- Burnt Umber
- Yellow Oxide
- Pthalo Blue
- Carbon Black
- Napthol Light Red
- Payne's Gray (Rowney Cryla Flow)
- Matt Medium (Rowney; gives a natural looking, semi-matt finish to bills, quills and legs)

ADDITIONS TO BASIC DIPPER PAINT KIT

Buy any other colours as you require them, but by the time you have collected the list that follows, you will be able to paint most subjects.

- Raw Umber (Liquitex)
- Payne's Gray
- Norwegian Orange
- Pine Green
- Pthalo Green
- Nimbus Gray
- Smoked Pearl
- Titanium White
- Warm White
- Opal
- Diox Purple

- Cadmium Yellow Light
- Neutral Gray (Liquitex, available in several shades)
- Flow Medium (makes paint more brushable, good for painting quills)
- Polyurethane Satin Finishing Varnish (the type for decoy carvers; a thinned coat gives a virtually undetectable matt finish and makes the paint surface more resistant to handling)
- Pearlescent powders (green, blue, white, violet, bronze)

COLOUR REFERENCE SYSTEM

Before painting your carving you will need to determine what colours you are going to use. You can work from photographs and magazines, but the colours are often inaccurate, especially in photographs taken in the early morning and evening, and it is difficult to pick out subtle variations in colour. You can average out your observations from photographs, but it is much better to work from a stuffed bird or, preferably, an unfaded, museum cabinet skin. The museum that I use lends out the skins, but many will only allow you to study them on the premises, and it is not always possible to get out your paints and try matching the colours. In that case some

Fig 10.4 The Dulux colour swatch can form the heart of a simple and cheap colour reference system.

other way of matching colours is required. Such a system is available in book form and is used by graphic artists, printers, and other professionals who require accurate colour reference material; the snag is that the books are expensive to produce and are made in relatively small numbers, so they are likely to cost in the region of £70 to £100. However, there is a very cheap solution available in the form of the colour swatches produced for computerized paint mixing machines, which are accurately produced in large numbers. I use a Dulux Colour Dimensions colour swatch book, containing approximately 800 different colours and shades, which I obtained from my local decorator's trade merchant. Because it is a computerized system, the colours are numbered in a logical way, making it possible to specify a colour between two printed colours, by number, if needed. It is possible to find the colour numbers that match museum specimens, make additional notes about colour sheens, feather edge colours and other variations, then leave the museum knowing that you have the necessary information to enable you to make a good job of painting your carving. When you have got the notes home, try and get to your paints as quickly as possible while the information is still fresh in your mind, and begin your trial paint mixes, keeping record cards.

TECHNIQUES

APPLYING AN UNDERCOAT

I use acrylic gesso as an undercoat on my carvings, and in the way I paint, I usually tint it with acrylic paints, to the lightest base colour on the bird. Coloured gesso is available, but probably the only useful colours for bird carvings would be dark brown or black, to undercoat any dark areas on the bird.

Thin the gesso so that it doesn't fill up the texturing as readily, and work it into the texturing with a large, stiff brush, finishing off with brush strokes in the direction of the surface texturing. Apply several thin coats to build up the depth of colour. Unlike the

washes, for which you can assist the drying with a hairdryer set on warm, allow each coat to dry naturally to avoid pin holes, caused where bubbles dry and burst.

UNDERPAINTING

Underpainting can be used to add depth and shading to feathers. For example, a Neutral Gray wash can be blended onto the gesso to darken the bases of the feathers, and when a colour wash is applied over this, the modelling of the feather will be improved. This is particularly useful when applied to areas of feathers which are basically one colour. It is possible, of course, to darken the base of a feather by blending a darker wash over the final colour, but this lacks the softening effect of a colour wash applied over it; underpainting gives a subtle effect, hard to achieve by blending the shading on top. Underpainting is often done with an airbrush, but they are rather expensive for occasional use.

WASH PAINTING

For wash painting, the paint is applied to the surface of the carving in very thin coats, and building up the colour sufficiently may take up to 20 thin washes of paint. Because a hairdryer can be used to dry each layer, and the next put on as soon as the surface is cool again, this process is not anywhere near as slow as it sounds. Make sure the surface

Thick paint will cover the peaks, but fill the troughs

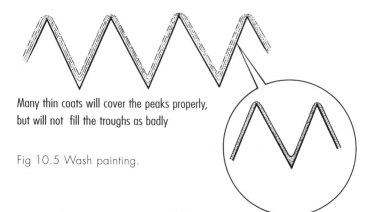

Many thin coats will cover the peaks properly, but will not fill the troughs as badly

Fig 10.5 Wash painting.

is cool before applying another wash or you may get instant drying, leaving brush marks which are very difficult to cover. Putting the paint on as thin washes ensures that the pigment is distributed over the surface in a much more even layer, and this helps retain the texturing: with thick layers of paint, there is more of a tendency for the pigment to gather in the grooves of the texturing, filling them up, whilst running off the peaks of the texture, leaving them thinly covered.

Add sufficient water to the paint to make a transparent wash which would need several coats to obliterate printing on white paper, but don't over-thin the paint with straight water, or the binding action of the acrylic polymer will be insufficient to prevent the pigment being rubbed off. Mix some matt medium in with the water when preparing very thin washes. The finished paint surface could also be given a coat of satin or matt finishing varnish to bind the pigment and protect it from handling. Use the largest brush that is available to get quick and even coverage of the surface when painting washes, but do not overload the brush or you will get puddles and runs forming. Blot excess paint from the brush with paper towel before you put it to the carving.

BLENDING

Methods of blending colour vary according to the situation; there are three methods of blending that I use.

METHOD 1 When blending different shades of the same colour, I blend them as washes directly on the bird, simply working one colour into the other. It is important that both colour areas are kept wet while you work, so I use two brushes, one for each shade.

METHOD 2 Two areas of colour laid side by side may be blended wet, by stippling the transition line between them with a soft blending brush. This can produce a muddy effect, especially with widely differing colours and I only use it occasionally, as I prefer method 3.

METHOD 3 The method I use most, because it can be used in just about any situation, is to blend colour to water – the method favoured by Jim Sprankle. When blending to water, one area is dampened (not wetted) with water, the wash is applied to the adjacent area, and a damp (not wet) brush used to soften the edge of the coloured area, drawing it slightly into the dampened one. After drying, the process can then be repeated in reverse if necessary. This method is easy to master as long as the areas you are blending are dampened and not wet. If they are wet, the paint will spread out and flow into the wet area uncontrollably. When building up colour depth with multiple washes, each wash must be blended in this way. Once mastered, this simple technique can be used to create very subtle effects.

AIRBRUSHING

If you happen to own an airbrush, you can use it to blend the base colours and to underpaint your bird. Like all tools, you get what you pay for; the cheapest airbrushes spray paint everywhere and are really no better than an aerosol spray can, and while the mid-priced ones are better, they still do not give the same precise control that the better ones have.

The best airbrushes give you complete control over the spray pattern and the

Fig 10.6
Airbrushes can be
run off cans of
propellant for
occasional use.

paint/propellant mix, and can even be used to spray very narrow lines. They require quite a lot of practice before you learn to control one properly though, and a good airbrush is expensive and needs careful maintenance. While a compressor is needed to run one, for very occasional use they can be run off inexpensive aerosol cans of propellant.

An airbrush, in my opinion, should only be used for underpainting and, possibly, blending colour on bills. Overuse leads to a dead, flat finish more like that seen on china figurines. I would not recommend a novice to go out and buy one, as they create more problems than they solve. A face mask should be worn, or better still, use an airbrushing booth whenever using an airbrush – paint particles breathed in can be dangerous. You should particularly avoid spraying pigments of cadmium and chrome, and keep the work area free of dried paint dust, which may be disturbed and released into the air.

SCRUBBING

This is a way of highlighting the top of the texturing by removing paint. After washes have been built up and are dry, but haven't had time to cure fully, scrub a dampened hog-bristle brush lightly over the surface of the texturing, then gently wipe with a damp paper towel to remove the loosened pigment. Done carefully, this will give you a lighter shade of the general colour; heavily executed, it will scrub through to the gesso!

Some artists wipe over the highlights with paper towel dampened with methylated spirits, but this is also rather vicious and likely to go through to the gesso or beyond! It can be used on fully cured paint though, where its action is slightly more controllable.

DRY BRUSHING

Another technique for highlighting the top of the texturing is to add colour. Take a stiff hog brush, load it with paint, blot most of the paint from it, and then brush it lightly over the texturing. This is rather more controllable than the previous method, as

the colour can be built up gradually. The brush must be very dry though, and leaving too much paint in the brush can cause you real problems.

FEATHER EDGING

Flicking feathers can be used to add a different colour to the tips of feathers, or to give the effect of individual feathers in areas of general texture, where individual feathers were not carved. This is a Jim Sprankle technique, and a special brush is required. (*See* Feather edging brushes, on page 81.) Load the paint into the brush with a sideways motion, like a cat swishing its tail, to help the brush keep its shape. When loaded, the fan-shaped brush takes up a shallow curve, and when touched lightly against the carving it leaves a curved, realistic feather edge. It does require time and practise to get it right though, and you have to train your own brush, but the results are impressive! Similar, but much slower results can be obtained by using individual strokes with a fine, well-pointed sable brush.

GLAZES

Glazes are used in the painting of bills and legs, to build up realistic, semi-translucent effects. Add a little colour to matt medium to form the glaze, and then treat it like a wash, and build it up in layers. The legs on the dipper, for example, have a thin red glaze over a white gesso base, which was then built up with thin gray glazes, blending in darkened areas as the layers were built up. The finished result is a translucent gray leg, with a hint of pink from the underlying blood vessels. (*See* page 106.) Glazes can also be used on feather quills to good effect.

ADDING IRIDESCENCE

The light refracting property of some birds' feathers gives them an iridescence which can be captured using a combination of two techniques. Washes of transparent colours can be built up over a very bright base colour to give a glowing effect, and this can be heightened by the addition of small amounts of special powders to the paints.

There are two types of these special powders available.

IRIDESCENT POWDERS These consist of dyed bronze and aluminium powders. I have found that these are not totally lightfast, and will be faded by strong light over a period of time.

PEARLESCENT POWDERS These mica-based powders get their colour from light refraction and are therefore unaffected by fading. The same powders are used in eye make-up, although make-up cannot be used in paint mixes.

VERMICULATION

This is the wavy line patterning which is apparent on the plumage of many ducks. It can be achieved in several ways, the most difficult to master being to paint them. Painting can be made easier by adding flow medium to the paint and using a very good quality, pointed, No 1 sable brush, but it is still quite hard to do.

A much easier way is to use a disposable, technical drawing pen, which can be bought in a variety of widths, but which are only available in black. The traditional, refillable technical drawing pen, however, can be filled with the liquid acrylic colours intended for use in airbrushes. There is a good range of these available, and they can be mixed, so this probably offers the best solution.

Watercolour pencils, which are available in a complete range of colours, can also be used to good effect. To make watercolour pencil or the ink of the disposable pens fast, spray the carving with a finishing varnish or fixative spray of some sort – do not brush it on or the pigment will run.

PALETTES

You will probably have used watercolour or poster colours at school, if not since. If so, you will know that paint which has dried on the palette can be re-wetted and made usable again. Because acrylic paints become insoluble once dry, care must be taken to

prevent the paint drying on the palette, as the dry paint may be broken up by the brush, and small flakes of dried paint transferred to the work. If these are not spotted and removed immediately, they can badly mar the finished paint surface. Two types of palette can be used to mix and work acrylics: a porous, damp palette, either commercial or home-made, or a solid, impervious palette.

Damp palettes can be bought or made up easily at home. To make your own, line a shallow plastic tray with several layers of damp kitchen towel or a layer of thin sponge, and cover this with a piece of greaseproof paper: colours are mixed with a brush on the greaseproof paper, and the moisture from the paper towel underneath prevents the thin layers of paint from drying out. If the palette is made up in a shallow, plastic, lidded box, the lid can be shut and the paint will remain usable for days. Alternatively, the tray can be kept in a plastic bag and this will have the same effect.

I favour the impervious type of palette, which allows mixing with a palette knife, and a slightly different way of working. Many people use a piece of plate glass placed over white card or paper, so that they can see the colour they are mixing; I prefer a pile of 6 x 6in (150 x 150mm), white ceramic wall tiles. I mix up the colour I need on a tile, and remove most of the mix, unthinned, to a 35mm film storage can, where it will keep for weeks. (Film cans can be scrounged from photo shops; try to get the translucent type so that you can see at a glance what colour they hold.) I thin the remaining paint to a wash for immediate use, topping up from the film can when necessary. To prevent any paint drying around the edge of the palette, I dampen it from time to time with a fine mist of water from a plastic pistol-grip spray container. If you have some colour on the palette which you need to keep from drying for a while, cover it with the plastic cap from an aerosol can. If you press some damp paper towel into the aerosol cap, the paint will stay workable for days. Several different tiles can be used at one time to prevent paints mixing together.

When I have finished with a tile palette, I throw it into a bucket of water which I keep by my side for washing brushes. The tiles clean up very easily after a soak in the bucket.

BRUSHES

Brushes, like paints, are expensive to buy initially, but they last a long while and do not all wear out at once. Buy the very best brushes that you can afford. People always tell you to buy the best tools you can afford, but this holds more true for brushes than any other tool I have ever used. I have tried all sorts of brushes, including some fairly expensive ones, but after attending a Jim Sprankle painting course, where I used the Raphael brushes he recommended, I have used nothing else. They are so well made and behaved that they are a real pleasure to use and worth paying a little more for. You can't cut down on the range of paints you need to get started, this is controlled by the project, but you can start with a minimum range of brushes, and add to this as you go along. My recommendations for a basic kit are based on painting the dipper and will cope well with the task: add the larger brushes for larger birds and the smaller ones as you feel them necessary.

GESSO BRUSHES
For applying gesso, you need a stiffer brush so that you can force the gesso down into the texturing, and for this, a bristle or hog-hair brush, of the type used in oil painting, is best. A ½in (12mm) flat will do to start with on smaller birds, but I also regularly use a ¾in (20mm) flat and ½ and ⅜in (12 and 10mm) rounds as well. As with washes, always try to use the largest possible brush to apply gesso – it helps to get the paint even. Don't overload the brush or you will be likely to get runs and to fill up the texturing, and make sure the final brush strokes follow the texture lines and do not cross them.

WASH BRUSHES
Synthetic hair brushes are made to mimic, as near as possible, the characteristics of the best natural hair, and most are suitable as wash painting brushes. I prefer them to the softer, mop-type, natural hair brushes used by many watercolour artists. I use synthetic, square-edged flats in widths of 1, ¾, ½, and ⅜in (25, 20 and 12mm). Again, if starting on smaller birds buy the ½ or ¾in (12 or 20mm) to start with. Always paint washes with the largest brush you can employ on the bird, and use a few long, even strokes rather than many short ones – this will help to prevent uneven application.

Raphael make some excellent small, synthetic, filbert brushes (these have a taper-pointed flat shape) in the 8204 series. Used flat they make good wash brushes on small areas, but turned edgeways, they become a very controllable, knife-shaped, detail brush. I use Nos 2, 4, and 6, but start with a No 4 if you are trying to keep down initial costs. The hair is very fine and can be damaged by over vigorous cleaning, so don't scrub them about too much.

DETAILING BRUSHES
Some detailing can be done with the small filbert brushes mentioned above, but I would add at least two more brushes to the basic kit.

The first would be a Raphael, 8224 series, No 2 lining brush. This long, synthetic brush can be used to paint quills, fine feather splits, and wispy hair-like feathers with great ease. For best effect, I use it in combination with Jo Sonja flow medium. Lining brushes are used to paint coach lines on carriages and cars and are also used by signwriters.

The second brush I would add would be a Raphael, 8408 series, No 1, watercolour round. These are beautifully shaped, pointed, Kolinsky sable brushes. I also use a No 2 and No 6 round sable, but they are expensive and I consider them a luxury! They keep their shape in use and will accurately put the paint where you want it – they are probably the most expensive of the brushes but they are a pleasure to use.

FEATHER-EDGING BRUSHES

To add interest and shape, the edges of feathers are often highlighted, or may even be painted a completely different colour. This effect can be produced laboriously with lots of short, fine, brush strokes, using a No 1 sable, or you can lay out some of your hard-earned cash and do it the way Jim Sprankle teaches. His method involves buying an expensive, long-haired, round, Kolinsky sable brush and abusing it by permanently flattening it out into a thin, fan shape. Don't get the idea that you can buy a fan or blending brush, or a cheaper, non-sable brush, because it just doesn't work.

To flatten the brush, load it with paint, and then scrape the paint out with the knife edge of a metal palette knife. Repeat this several times, wash the brush out and flatten it again. Always flatten the brush from the same side – I do it with the writing on the handle uppermost, as this makes it easy to check that I do have it facing the same way. Always store the brush upright, and before storing it, moisten your fingers with saliva to dampen the bristles, and then flatten the brush again: when the saliva dries it will keep the brush in shape. Treated regularly like this, the brush will eventually start to take up a permanent set. Never try to use it as a round brush again, or you will totally ruin the brush.

To train a brush in this way, you need a long series, Kolinsky sable brush: a Raphael, 8404 series, Nos 2 and 6, will make a pair that cover most needs, but they are expensive, and you will need strong nerves!

BLENDING BRUSHES

There are three methods by which colours can be blended, one of which needs a special type of brush. Blending colours wet to wet entails laying down two colours side-by-side, and then gently stippling the interface, to blend the colours into each other. You can make a brush for this by taking a fairly cheap squirrel or ox hair, No 6 or 8 round brush, and trimming the point off square, to about half the original length; it can then be used like a stencil brush to blend the transition line. You may also need to make a smaller brush.

CLEANING AND CARING FOR BRUSHES

Having invested in good quality brushes, look after them; never lend your good brushes to anyone, they are too easily ruined, and keep them hidden away from children! Never allow paint to dry in a brush, as the paint is then waterproof and extremely difficult to remove without ruining the brush. When changing colours, or when you have finished using a brush, remove the excess paint on a rag or paper towel before giving the brush a good rinse in water. I keep a bucket for this, half filled with water, as you can be much more vigorous with the rinsing than by using the usual jam jar. As mentioned previously, I also use the bucket to throw my used tile palettes into for later cleaning. I have a jam jar containing clean water on my bench and the brush gets a second rinse in this. If the water in the jam jar is kept clean, by regular changing, you will see if the brush still contains any paint. If it does, I use an old bar of soap, drawing the brush across it and working the soap into the brush head, before going back to the bucket and repeating the process.

If you need to leave a brush for more than a few moments and don't have time to clean it, don't leave it standing on its bristles in water, leave it suspended. You can buy artists' water cans with a coiled spring to clip the brush handle in, or you could use a makeshift arrangement, like a card cover for your jam jar, with a central hole to take the brush, and a bulldog clip to hold the brush handle.

When I have finished with the brushes for the day, I always wash them with soap and warm water, dry them with paper towel, then use my fingers moistened with saliva to re-shape the brush before storing it upright in a jar. Don't lick the brush directly to re-point it, as many pigments are derived from substances which are poisonous, such as cadmium or lead.

Well looked after, a set of good brushes will last several years, and replacements will only have to be bought occasionally.

PROJECTS AND PATTERNS

Carving the dipper serves as a good basic introduction to the different specialized aspects of bird carving. This project is covered in great detail and with many photographs, so that all stages of production are clear. This British dipper really only varies from its northern European and American cousins in its colouring.

The green woodpecker, the second project, is a purely European subject, and presents some slightly different problems.

The final project, the common tern, is found throughout the northern hemisphere. The design is almost a decoy duck, but with more challenging wing, tail and head carving – it makes a very lively and animated looking bird.

Although each successive project is described in less detail, the specific problem areas are highlighted, and the project is photographed at various stages throughout the carving and painting. If you are unsure about any of the techniques used, please refer back to the relevant chapter in the first section of the book, where techniques and materials are explained in detail.

A selection of drawings for further projects is also included, with not a duck in sight!

Left: Great spotted woodpecker
(*Dendrocopos major*).

CHAPTER 11

DIPPER

THE SUBJECT

Clean, shallow, stony upland rivers and
streams are the habitat of this enchanting,
dumpy, wren-like bird. They are a regular
feature of a walk in the Yorkshire Dales
where I live. They have a delightful song,
and may often be seen perched on a
rock in mid-stream, bobbing or dipping up
and down. They are, as far as I know,
unique amongst aquatic birds in not having
any webs between the toes. The bird
described here is the English white and
ginger breasted variety, *Cinclus cinclus*;
the northern European birds lack the
gingery breast feathers, as does the
American dipper, *Cinclus mexicanus*, which
is similar, but has entirely grey-brown
plumage.

The dipper is a good project for a first
foray into bird carving; a popular bird, its
simple, strong shape makes it a delightful
and not too complex carving, and the
almost monotone plumage provides a
straightforward introduction to painting for
the newcomer.

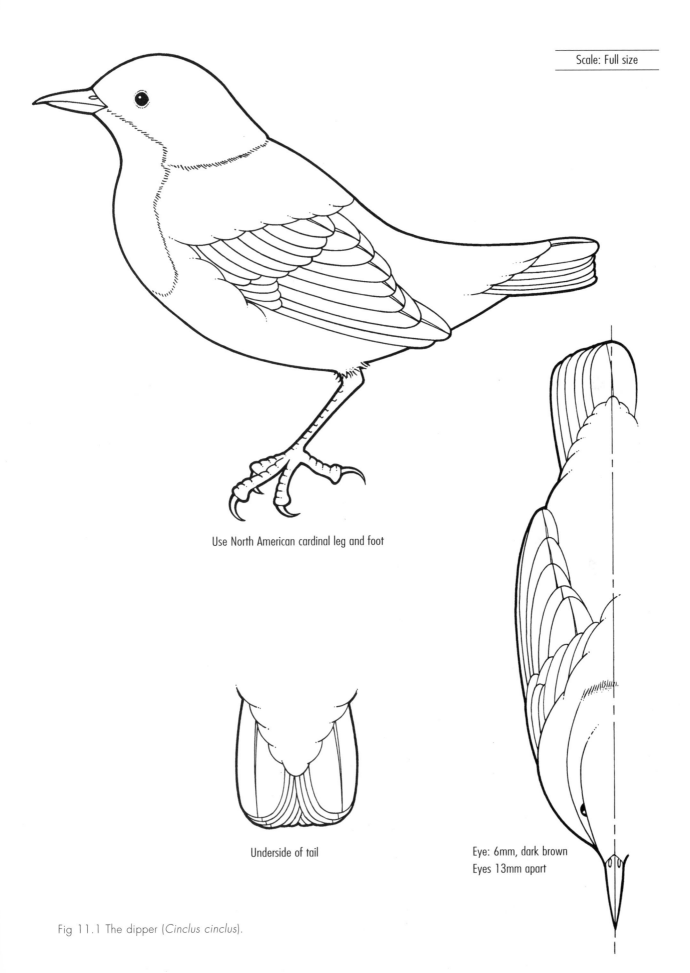

Scale: Full size

Use North American cardinal leg and foot

Underside of tail

Eye: 6mm, dark brown
Eyes 13mm apart

Fig 11.1 The dipper (*Cinclus cinclus*).

THE BASIC CONCEPT AND DESIGN

The habits of any bird are the main source of ideas for carvings. The dipper is usually spotted, bobbing up and down on a rock at the edge of a stream, then flying off at high speed, frantically beating its short wings. Occasionally it will be seen singing a surprisingly melodious song whilst standing on its rock, and in the breeding season it may appear with a mouthful of caddis larvae, checking that all is clear before flying to its nest. A flying bird is not really an option for a first project, so mounting the bird on a rock or rocks is an obvious choice. The dipping action is fairly hard to convey in a carving: because it is a complete cycle of movement, if stopped mid-way, the carving will be short of clues as to the complete action. Impending flight is a little easier to imply, and in addition, turning and tilting the head can convey the impression of searching or listening. Adding a beak full of caddis larvae would complete another possible scenario, which is only a little more difficult to carve, if you are feeling confident.

Having developed a basic idea, this needs to be turned into an actual design. The dipper's simple, strong shape makes a delightful carving which doesn't require anything very elaborate to display it. The bird can be carved directly from the drawing, looking straight ahead, or, depending on your confidence and ability, the pattern can be redrawn to create a different, more lively pose. More action and a hint of a story can be added to what otherwise might be a fairly lifeless portrait.

The bird is portrayed as if about to fly off down the river, ever so slightly off balance, to help create the illusion of impending movement. This effect needs to be subtle; overdone, the bird will just look like it is falling flat on its beak! The dipper will also appear alert – maybe something has disturbed it, prompting the flight. Turning the head will help convey this impression, and the head could also be cocked to one side. Combining these two factors gives the basis for the design.

The basic drawing work on the dipper has already been carried out for you, although if you have access to any first-hand information, checking it against the drawings would still be a good idea. The design was based on several photographs, a C. F. Tunnicliffe painting, and two study skins from Cliffe Castle Museum at Keighley in Yorkshire.

Spending some time making a Plasticine maquette of the bird will allow you to develop the pose further before arriving at a final working pattern. (*See* Maquettes in Chapter 5, on page 42.) The time spent will not be wasted, as carving will proceed much quicker with a maquette to follow, and hopefully, a much more animated bird will be carved than if work proceeded straight from the drawing.

MARKING OUT AND BANDSAWING THE BLANK

Prepare the cardboard pattern from the drawing or maquette, with extra material added around the beak, tail and wing tips, and use this to mark out a block of timber at least $\frac{1}{4}$in (6mm) larger all round than the pattern.

Align the patterns and use a felt-tip pen to trace around them onto the clean, squared timber block (*see* Chapter 6).

Fig 11.2 The patterns are aligned and transferred onto the squared timber.

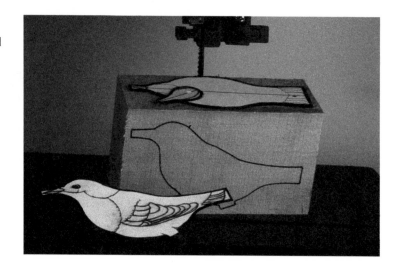

Carefully cut the side profile to the outside of the pencil line, and then use the waste pieces from the side profile to support the blank whilst cutting the top view. Always try to keep the waste as two complete pieces, so that it is easier to reassemble them to form a block again for the next cut. Glue from a hot melt glue gun is good for reassembly, and masking tape is a good alternative.

When you have reassembled the block, carefully cut around the top profile to reveal a chunky bird-like shape. If you have decided to carve the bird with its head turned, refer to Roughing out a turned head in Chapter 6 for more detailed instructions and photographs.

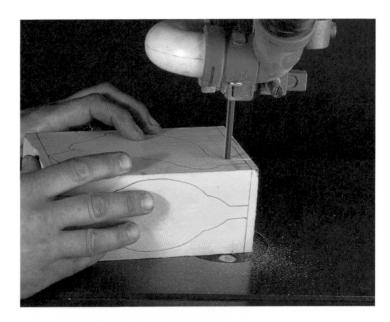

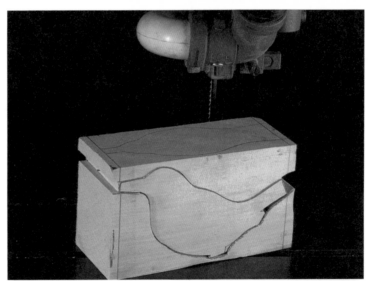

Fig 11.3 After drawing around the patterns for both side and top, the side profile is carefully cut out.

Fig 11.4 The waste pieces from cutting the first profile are used to support the blank whilst cutting the top view.

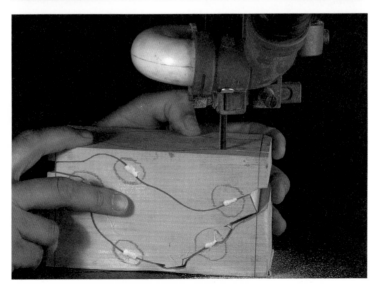

Fig 11.5 Cutting the top profile on the reassembled block.

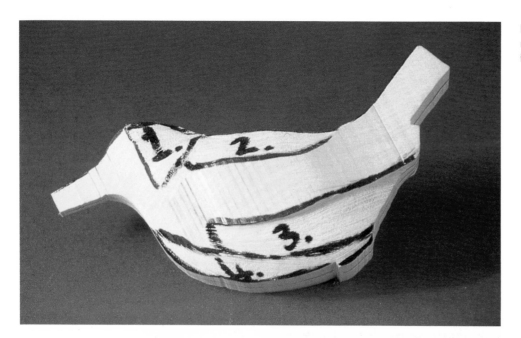

Fig 11.6 Wood is removed from these four areas first.

INITIAL ROUGHING OUT OF THE BLANK

The first operation in roughing out is to remove the bulk of the waste from the bandsawn blank so that the proper bird-like shape can begin to emerge. The angular blank often only vaguely resembles a bird, especially if the head has been turned away from the body centre-line. Turning the head gives it odd, angular projections which need to be corrected before you permanently incorporate them into the carving! I always draw centre-lines and once this is done, remove wood from four main areas.

THE BACK OF THE HEAD, WHERE IT MEETS THE BODY The back of the head profile is the full width of the body on the newly cut blank, so cut two blocks of waste away from the shoulder areas to define the area which will become the head.

THE BACK Remove the sharp corners along the back of the bird, from the shoulder area back towards the tail, at an angle of about 45°: this area will be rounded over later.

THE SIDES Sketch in the lower line of the wing, and reduce the thickness of the area below it, from full width at the shoulder, going deeper as the cut moves back towards the tail.

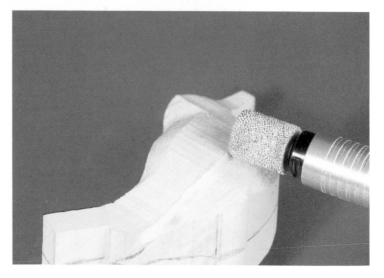

THE BREAST AND BELLY Finally, remove the sharp corners from the breast and belly areas in the same way as described for the back.

I did all the initial roughing out for this project with a cylindrical carbide cutter, but any suitable tool can be used and many carvers like to use a knife. Removing the sharp corners like this makes it easier to sketch in the details for the next steps, otherwise they make it difficult to draw smooth connecting lines across the surface of the carving. Removing the initial waste also helps you to visualize the finished shape.

Fig 11.7 The initial roughing out was performed with a cylindrical carbide cutter.

WINGS AND TAIL

The carving has its shape refined in stages, each one incorporating more detail than the last, slowly bringing the carving to completion.

Once the initial waste is removed, draw in the outlines of the wings, and upper and lower tail. With the upper tail and wing areas marked out, they can now be shaped up a bit more, though at this stage it is still only the basic shape that is being formed.

Make sure that the surfaces 'flow' from one area of the bird to another; the shape needs to be cohesive, with no areas joined awkwardly to the adjacent ones. Reveal the lower tail area by removing the waste from between the wings, then form the vent channel feather groups, making sure that the overall curve of the belly through to the under tail coverts is a smooth one. This can be carried out with hand tools or, if power carving, a flame-shaped, fine carbide burr, or bud-shaped ruby carver.

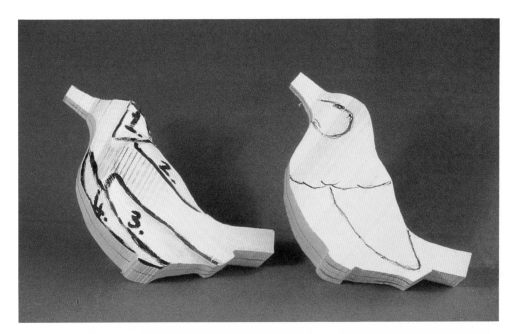

Fig 11.8 After removing the initial waste areas, the wings, upper and lower tail areas, and other major details are sketched in.

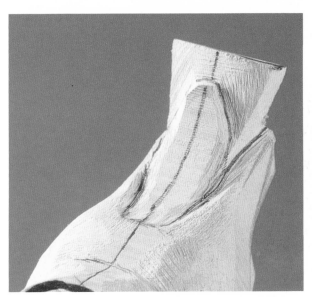

Fig 11.9 The upper tail and wing areas are now shaped a bit more.

Fig 11.10 The lower tail, the area between the wing tips, and the vent channel are also roughed out.

FEATHER CARVING

Before laying out the feathers in pencil, I give the roughed-out blank a light sanding, as this gives a better surface for marking out. After sanding, I carefully draw the wing and tail feathers onto the blank. I do this at an early stage as I find it helps in the visualization of the piece as you work on it. The feathers can't be traced from the drawing, as the surface they are to cover is curved and hence larger than that shown on the drawing. The easiest way to draw them is to establish the relative positions of the feather tips with a light pencil line, and then draw out the feathers so that they fill all the available wing surface. When you have drawn the feathers on the wings, identify the main feather groups, and relieve around their edges to form a small step; this allows them to be carved overlapping the group below. A small sanding drum or fine, cylindrical carbide burr are best for this job, although it would be possible to use a small gouge. Where the pencil lines have been carved away, they will need to be redrawn in readiness for the actual feather carving.

The hard-edged feathers of the wing and tail can be outlined using a knife or pyrograph to form a stop cut, then carefully

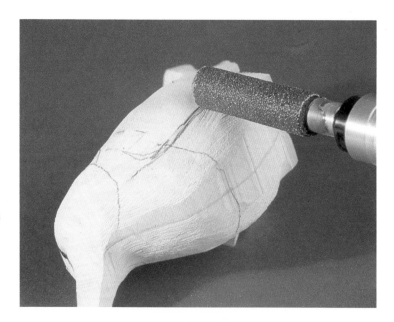

Fig 11.11 The roughed-out blank is lightly sanded to give a better surface for laying out the feathers in pencil.

carved, to give the impression of overlap, with a knife or small skew chisel, or as I often do, with a safe-ended, cylindrical diamond burr. Using the diamond cutter gives a slightly more uneven edge to the feathers.

When carving the wings, and particularly the tail, I try to create an illusion of thinness, whilst maintaining plenty of strength. I expect my carvings to end up in a domestic environment rather

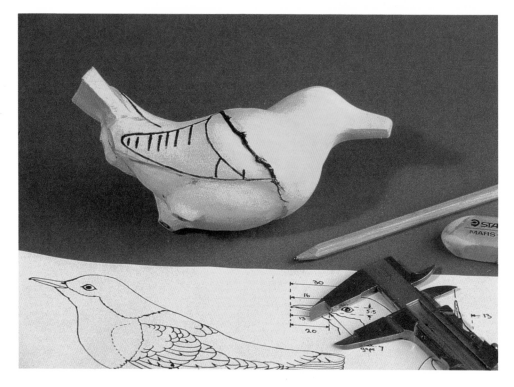

Fig 11.12 The overall shape of the wing is established, and the feather tip positions are marked out from the drawing.

Fig 11.13 The feathers have now been drawn in to completely cover the wing surface.

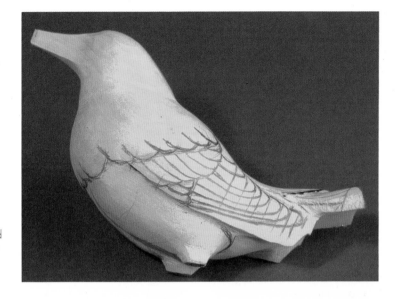

Fig 11.14 A cylindrical burr or sanding drum is used to relieve the feather groups on the wing surface.

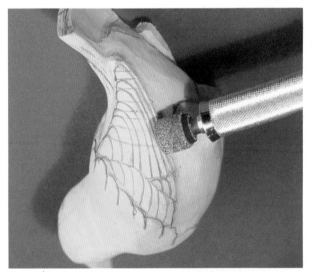

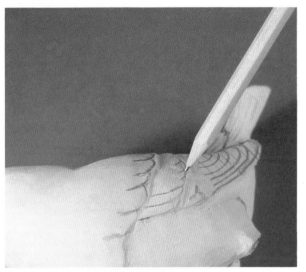

Fig 11.15 The pencil indicates where the feather groups have been relieved.

Fig 11.16 After sanding up the newly carved feather groups, the pencilled feather outlines are reinstated.

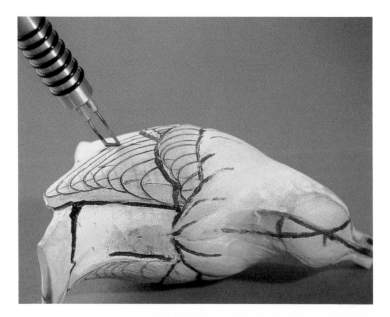

than a museum, so I allow for the increased likelihood of damage. Although when viewed from most angles it isn't noticeable, the dipper's tail is almost ¼in (6mm) thick in the centre, but the edges of individual feathers look thin, because of the shaping and slight undercutting.

The pyrograph is used to clean up corners and awkward areas when carving feathers. Make sure you are familiar with the layout of the feathers, so that you know which areas should overlay what – this causes much confusion for novice bird carvers. If you want to incorporate feather splits to add more interest, they need to be planned before carving the feather, as they modify the feather outline.

Fig 11.17 The pyrograph is used to form a stop cut around each hard-edged feather outline.

Fig 11.18 A small skew chisel is used to cut away wood from the top edge of each feather, to give the impression of overlap.

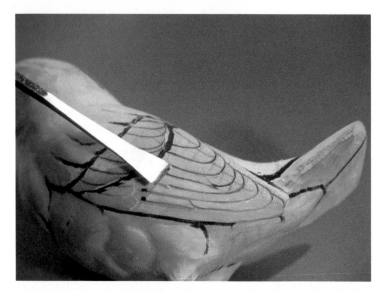

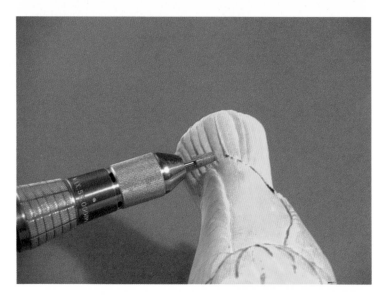

Fig 11.19 Carving the tail feathers using a cylindrical diamond cutter.

FEATHER CLUMPS AND GROUPS

My birds have a characteristic fluffy, or even muscled appearance. To give the bird this more fluffed up appearance and disguise the basic feathered, egg-shaped body which would otherwise result, I break up the whole surface of the bird into clumps and groups of feathers. In reality, birds may often look smoother, like a feathered egg in fact, but realism in a carving is often achieved through the exaggeration of certain features.

Whilst hard, distinctly defined feathers are to be found on the wings and tail, the other feathers on a bird have soft and often almost indistinguishable outlines: forming feather groups and clumps adds more variety to the surfaces clad with these soft-edged feathers. I treat the whole bird, excepting its tail, wings and head, in this way. I leave the head until the carving of the bill and eye areas is complete, and on small birds, I texture the crown of the head without carving mounds of feathers first.

Feather clumps can be formed with a gouge, and then softened by sanding, so that they blend into each other. Alternatively, a ball-shaped ruby or diamond cutter can be used, followed by sanding with a sanding mandrel, and then sanding by hand.

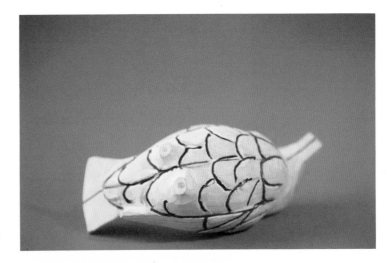

Fig 11.20 Feather groups are drawn onto the soft feather areas of the body.

Fig 11.21 The soft feather groups on the body have been carved and shaped with a ball-shaped ruby carver.

Whichever way you choose, the effect needs to be subtle, one clump 'melting' into the next with no distinct separation. It is also important that the feather clumps are not too regular, as this will give a stuffed, patchwork toy appearance.

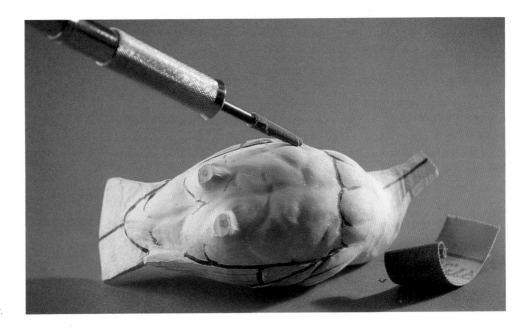

Fig 11.22 Sanding the soft feather groups with a cartridge roll sander.

HEAD

With the wing and tail feathers carved, more work can be carried out on the head, starting with a correction of overall shape and size. I often do this using a knife instead of the grinder – it gives a change of pace, and time to reflect and study the shape better. I then start to form the cheek and eye grooves; by deepening the eye grooves evenly I almost achieve the correct eye to eye distance, and then I narrow the area above the eye groove, blending it into the crown. I don't work on the beak at this stage, as it would then be vulnerable to damage, but leave it as a rectangular projection.

INITIAL BILL SHAPING

Carefully mark out the bill on the rectangular projection left for it, then reduce the size of the bill block so that the front of the head can be finally shaped, redrawing as the work continues: shape the bill a little oversize initially.

FIXING THE EYE POSITION

The eye positions can now be determined. Draw a line from eye centre to bill tip on one side of the head, and mark on the eye centre, positioned along this line. You will have to determine the actual position of the eye centre empirically, referring to the bill/head intersection and the top of the head. I always check my reference pictures carefully – it is important that the head looks right as it becomes the main focus point on the bird.

When happy with the eye position on one side of the head, transfer it to the other, using two pointed awls or compass points. To do this, push one awl into the timber at the determined eye position, perpendicular to the axes of the head, and hold the second awl lightly against the other side of the head. Align the awls visually from the front and from above, and when happy with the alignment, mark the wood with the second awl. Drill the eye holes separately from each side, but if they are drilled perpendicular to the head axes, they should meet in the

Fig 11.23 Marking out the head and bill from the drawing.

middle. This is a surprisingly accurate way of marking out, but an easy alignment check to carry out after drilling, is to put a length of dowel, or twist a drill of the correct diameter, right through the eye hole, and then check the alignment again, from above and in front of the head. If one eye doesn't align properly, enlarge the hole slightly at one side or pull the hole over using a tapered ruby carver.

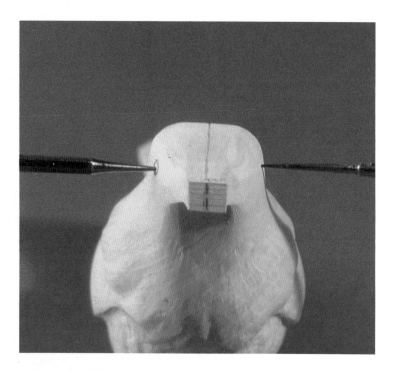

Fig 11.24 Transferring the eye position from one side of the head to the other for drilling. Note the slight misalignment of the points, which is easy to detect using this method.

FINISHING THE BILL

Further shaping of the head and final carving of the bill can now be carried out, paying particular attention to where the bill meets the featherline. Use fine, abrasive burrs and stones so that work proceeds slowly and manageably — too much removed at this stage is a disaster to avoid! After sanding with fine wet-and-dry paper, use the pyrograph to tidy up the featherline, and to form the separation between the upper and lower parts of the bill. When all of this is done, soak the finished bill tip with thin superglue to toughen it; this treatment can be used on any thin and vulnerable areas, but only after all work has been completed, as the fumes given off when it is heated are toxic.

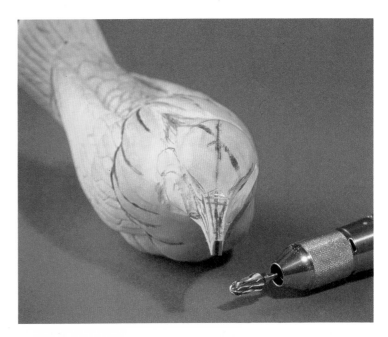

Fig 11.25 Refining the head and bill shape using a carbide burr.

Fig 11.26 The head shape is developing, and the rectangle of wood left to carve the bill can be seen.

Fig 11.27 The head is shaped and the bill carved, ready for detailing.

TEXTURING HARD-EDGED FEATHERS

With all the shaping of the bird complete, the final surface texture of feathers can be commenced. Complete the hard-edged feathers first, as they all meet, and are overlapped by soft feather areas.

QUILLS

Where quills are showing, form them first. For fine quills burn two lines with the pyrograph pen, holding it at a shallow angle to the feather surface, and burning a line from each side. Carve and sand the heavier quills individually. Make all the quills curve gently – they are never ramrod straight – and do try not to make them too heavy, especially where they reach the tip of the feather. Most quills are almost indiscernible at the tip, so a single burn line at that point will suffice.

BASE TEXTURE

At this point the hard-edged feathers should be sanded smooth, but if they have feather barb lines burned on them now, the smooth, even surface will show when the bird is painted – this is because of the way the smooth wood surface catches the light. A softer, more matt look can be achieved by first texturing that smooth surface to give a series of small undulations which will scatter the light more unevenly. Where the stone runs over the edge of the feather, it softens the hard, tile-like edge and improves the appearance of the feather. This texturing can be carried out with a small, smooth, ball-shaped abrasive stone, and if the feather is sufficiently large, a larger stone can be used to form ripples on the feather surface as well. A reversible grinder is most useful for this as you can prevent wood fibres from being torn up by selecting the grinder direction to suit the grain.

I follow this base texturing with a home-made sanding and de-fuzzing wheel, consisting of several 1¼in (32mm), fine, Scotchbrite discs on a mandrel, run at a very slow speed. This leaves a silky smooth

surface to burn on. Very fine cloth-backed abrasive or wet-and-dry paper could be used for this as well.

BARB LINES

Burn the feather barb lines with the pyrograph pen held perpendicular to the surface of the feather, so that the finest lines can be burned as close together as possible.

Fig 11.28 Burning feather markings onto the hard-edged feathers.

I burn several times usually, firstly with the pen on a cool setting, completely covering the feather surface with tightly spaced lines, then again with some lines at higher heat settings. The hotter the pen, the wider the line it burns, and the coarser the effect; large feathers tend to have less lines per inch than small feathers. One or two wider lines give the appearance of fine feather splits, but any proper splits, which will actually alter the feather outline, will have been carved earlier. Try to vary the angle of the burning lines slightly from feather to feather, as well as curving them, to stop one feather merging into the next. Hard-edged feathers can also be undercut with the pyrograph to give more separation of the feathers, but beware that this leaves the edge of the feather more vulnerable to damage, especially if overheated with the pyrograph, which makes the timber more brittle. I try to vary the combination of techniques used to suit the particular bird and area of feathers.

It is important that the feather barbs, as well as the quills, are curved, or else the feathers will look like Christmas trees. Keep as much of the burning pen in contact with the feather surface as the work will allow: don't just use the point, as the pen will run in its own track, like an ice skate, keeping the lines smooth. A curve can be induced by ever so slightly rolling the pen between thumb and fingers as you move it across the surface. Practise on some scrap first, and always try to start work on a less noticeable part of a carving, while your rhythm and technique gets into gear! Study some real feathers and you will see that the barbs look like a flat 'S'; this is very difficult to master, and usually so subtle that you will get away with a simple uni-directional curve.

The temperature you need the pen set at will depend on the qualities of the timber and the speed at which you burn the lines. If you burn slowly, a wider, heavier line will result than one burned quickly, with the pyrograph set at the same temperature. This effect can be used to produce shading, by burning slowly away from the quill, and speeding up towards the edge of the feather. Be careful not to nick or cut across the quill as it will show when painted, but equally, the burn line must start right against the quill; many carvers use a headband magnifier to assist them in achieving this.

Hone the burning pen in the same way as a knife, to keep it sharp and clean; mine will easily slice through a sheet of writing paper. I use chrome cleaner on a leather-faced block, but let the tip cool first! Don't use wet-and-dry paper, as recommended in some books, or you will rapidly wear away the pen, and they are not cheap to replace!

TEXTURING SOFT FEATHERS

Before texturing the soft feather areas on the underside of the bird, you need to drill the holes to take the legs, and carve the feather tufts around them. The stubs which form the leg tufts have been left oversize to make drilling easier. Fit the correct size drill to a small, hand-held electric drilling machine or the handpiece of the flexi-shaft, then carefully align the drill bit and start the hole, stopping to check the alignment of the drill to the body. Check from the front and the side of the bird, and if it is alright, carry on with the drilling. If it isn't, pull the hole into line as you drill. The leg tufts can now be safely carved down to size, ready for texturing with the other soft feather areas.

Soft feather areas are textured using abrasive stones. Different sizes and shapes of stone make different texturing marks, and these can be used to build up a texture. Soft feather areas can be carved as individual feathers or as an overall, soft, feathery texture. I use a series of flattish curves or 'S' shapes to create a soft feather texture, but the overall effect relies upon the complete surface of the bird being thoroughly textured, sometimes with three or four different layers.

Firstly, I pencil feather flow lines onto the carving, over all the areas of the bird, to establish the direction that the texturing will run in each different area. I then build up the texture in layers. For the first layer, I go over each area loosely with wider, coarser lines, I then follow this with a more thorough layer using a stone which gives a medium line, and finally, give a very thorough, overall texture with a very fine stone. Each stone leaves a different texturing line, so more variety and interest is added as the surface texture builds up. For the final texturing, I follow the feather flow lines, to establish a visual flow over the surface of the bird. The hair-like feathers, found particularly on the heads of some birds, I burn with a pyrograph, over a lightly stoned base texture.

Fig 11.29 Drilling
the holes for the
legs.

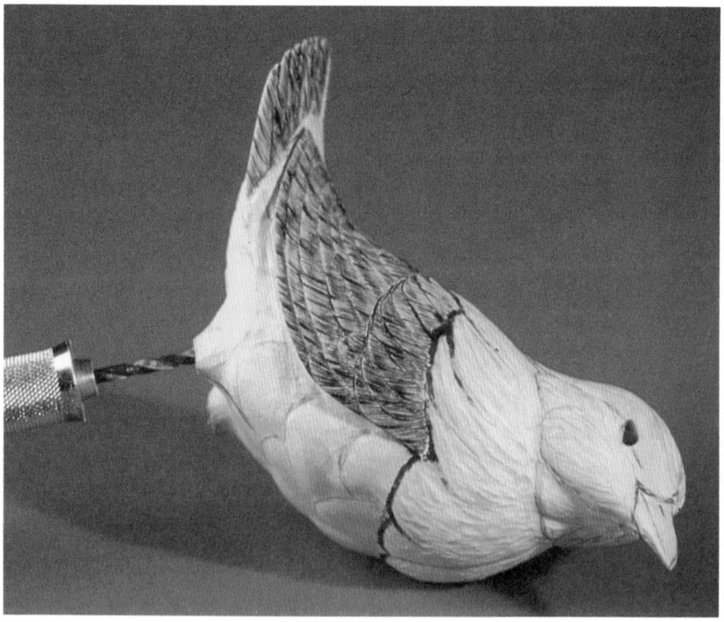

Fig 11.30 The flow
of feathers over the
soft feather areas.

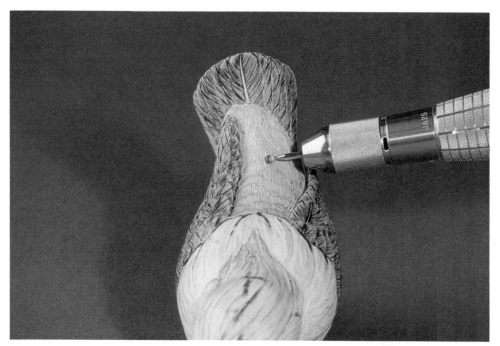

Fig 11.31 Using a
small texturing stone
to create the texture
on the soft feather
areas.

Fig 11.32 Four views of the almost completed carving.

BASE

I sketched my original composition for the dipper with the carving mounted on a single stone with a sloping side to take the bird, confident that I could carve a suitable stone to fit later. Carving a wooden rock sounds simple, but for the greatest success and realism, you do need to study how rocks weather and split: for this purpose I keep quite a few nice water-worn stones that I

Fig 11.33 Natural rocks arranged as a base for the bird.

have picked up from time to time. Rather than put one stone on a wooden base with the bird on top, I changed my idea slightly and found three flattish, striated stones that made a pleasing arrangement, which was in harmony with the bird.

CARVING THE ROCKS

To carve the rocks, I traced around them, and cut out appropriate thicknesses of jelutong. I then shaped them roughly on a disc sander, before dowelling the three 'rocks' together: I waited until they were carved and painted before gluing them. I didn't aim to copy the stones exactly as I carved them, but used the general shapes, and how they had split and worn, to create wooden versions that could have been picked up next to them. To carve the rocks I used a cylindrical, tungsten carbide burr and a carbide rotor saw.

Once I had shaped and coarsely sanded them, I charred them thoroughly with a blowlamp; this softens the rocks and takes off the corners as though they were water worn. I then brushed off the charred wood with a fine brass brush, and used sandpaper for a final cleaning up, and to lighten all the highpoints. To finish, I gave the timber a coat of sealer.

When they had dried, I coated the stones with PVA woodworking glue and covered them with dry silver sand. This process was repeated when the first coat had dried, and when the second coat was dry, I applied a thinned coat of adhesive to bond any loose sand particles.

PAINTING

Silver or silica sand is fairly transparent, so the darker areas of charring which were not sanded away, already gave some depth and shading to the stones, leaving only a few washes of earth colours to complete the painting. When the paint was dry, I glued the three stones together to form the base; they touch only lightly, leaving a space between them, which adds nicely to the overall composition.

LEGS

There is a good range of American cast metal feet available, and for this carving I used a pair designed for a cardinal, made by a company called Delise. The lengths of the leg and toes corresponded with the study skins I had measured and the leg was also the correct thickness. Glue the legs into the body using five minute epoxy adhesive, and set them on the base to dry in the correct position; do not glue them to the base until after painting. When the glue has cured, place a small ring of epoxy ribbon putty around the top of the leg, and use it to blend the leg tuft to the leg. Use a pointed dental tool or wire to texture and draw out the putty; dipping the tool into a piece of Plasticine will keep it from sticking to the putty.

Fig 11.34 Blanks cut out and dowelled to carve the base.

Fig 11.35 Base after carving and burning.

EYES

Before texturing the head, try the eyes in their sockets to make sure that they are not too tight a fit, and that they can be positioned correctly. Once this is done, soften the corners of the eye holes by sanding, and then texture the head right up to the eye hole, using the same variety of abrasive stones used to build up texture on the soft feather areas.

Fit the eyes on a bed of epoxy putty. I use the stick type putty which can be smoothed with water, and which will be displaced around the eye as it is pushed in and positioned. Push the eye in and adjust it with the eraser end of a pencil – this won't slip or scratch the glass. Scrape away the excess putty which is forced out around the eye (I use an old dental tool for this), so that the eye is unobscured when checking the final position. Dark brown eyes with small black pupils or black bead eyes can be used. With most small birds' eyes, unless they are a bright colour like white, red or yellow, I fit black bead eyes.

If coloured, flat-backed eyes or convex/concave eyes are used, they should be fitted with the back of the eye perpendicular to the vertical axis of the head, but tilted inwards towards the front to make the bird look forward. Properly fitted eyes should not look startled – if the eyes won't go in deep enough, the hole is too small. As a general rule, when viewed from the back of the head the eyes should be obscured, observed from the top, they may be just visible, and when seen directly from the front they should stare straight back at you.

EYE RINGS

Make the eye ring from a small roll of epoxy ribbon putty – this is not the same as used to set the eye, but the type used on the leg tufts. Roll out with your fingertips, on a small piece of acrylic plastic. Rubbing a lump of Plasticine over the plastic and over your fingers will prevent the putty sticking. (*See* Eye rings in Chapter 9, on page 66.) Arrange the roll of epoxy putty around the eye, fixing it by carefully using a pointed dental tool to squash and draw the putty from the outer edge of the ring into the texturing. If it is fixed in one or two places first, minor adjustments can be made to the shape of the eye ring before finishing it. Look at reference photographs to determine how the eye ring looks.

The finished eye ring can be textured using a small metal tube or dental tool. I use an assortment of hypodermic needles of varying sizes, with the points stoned flat. These can be pressed lightly into the surface to give a knobbly texture to the eye ring.

Fig 11.36 The base is finished, the eyes are fitted, and the carving is ready to seal for painting.

Fig 11.37 For painting, the carving can be fixed to a wooden block . . .

PAINTING

CLEANING AND SEALING

When the putty on the eye rings is dry, carefully brush out all the texturing and burning lines over the whole bird, using a soft, nylon rotary brush run at low speed. (Epoxy putty takes about 24 hrs to dry, and plastic wood about 3–4 hrs). Both should be left to dry naturally. The brushing must be done along the texture lines, not across them, as this could break off thin areas of texturing.

The carving is then temporarily fixed to a wooden block or wooden painting stick, so that it can be easily held and worked on. I use the smallest drop of superglue to hold the legs into the wood, and split the wood away when painting is complete. The peg end of the leg could also be held in a large pin vice.

When thoroughly brushed, give the carving two or three coats of cellulose sanding sealer thinned with an equal amount

Fig 11.38 . . . or painting stick.

of thinners. Use a fairly stiff brush to apply thin coats, following the lines of texturing, and being careful not to allow it to run or puddle, as any build-up will hide the surface detail.

Once the sealing has dried, give the carving a final brush, to remove any remaining wood fibres. (Sealer takes only about 15 mins to dry. Apply the sealer in an area where there is good ventilation.)

APPLYING THE UNDERCOAT

Thin the gesso (mix A) to the consistency of thin cream and paint the bird with a stiff, hog bristle brush, working the gesso down into the texturing, and finishing off with brush strokes following the texture lines. Allow the gesso to dry naturally, as hastening the drying with heat tends to leave pinholes which you cannot get paint to cover later. Several coats will be needed to completely cover the bird, but once you have got complete coverage, you can assist the drying of further coats with a cool hair dryer.

Fig 11.39 After sealing, the carving is given a final brush to remove remaining wood fibres.

COLOUR MIXES

MIX A
Gesso undercoat

MIX B
Golden brown band between chest and belly

MIX C
Chocolate brown on head

24 parts white acrylic gesso to 1 part Raw Umber

8 parts Raw Sienna to 5 parts Burnt Sienna to 1 part Burnt Umber

10 parts Raw Umber to 2 parts Yellow Oxide to 1 part white acrylic gesso

MIX D
Blue-black on wings, tail, back and rump

2 parts Pthalo Blue to 1 part Carbon Black

MIXING TIP Mix A is used first, though some of it can be stored in a small, sealed container for touch-up and detailing later. The three other pre-determined base colours can be pre-mixed and stored in 35mm film containers: minor variations can be carried out by applying thin washes of various colours over these, on the actual carving.

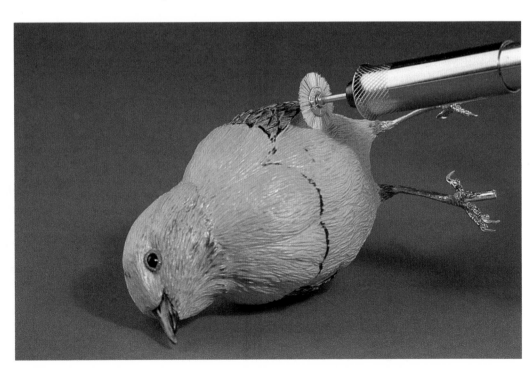

APPLYING THE COLOURS

Plan out the areas of colour on the carving with very thin, transparent washes of the base colours. The advantage of doing this is that you can immediately get a feel for how it is going to look when the painting is finished. An alternative system is to use a watercolour pencil to mark out the colour areas. As long as this is done lightly with a sharp pencil, the tiny amount of watercolour pigment will be lost in the washes, and any that isn't painted over can be removed with clean water and a brush after the acrylic has dried.

Paint the golden band between the chest and belly first (mix B), drawing some of the colour up to form splits in the white chest area and give a slightly ragged interface between the colours. Build the colour up as a series of fairly thin washes, drying with a hair dryer between coats. The dryer can be used hot, but the paint must be allowed to cool before applying the next coat.

I wet blended the two different browns (mix B and mix C) directly on the bird, but a novice would find it easier to dampen (not wet!) one area with clean water and blend one colour into that, then reverse the process, using the other colour. It sounds complicated, but it isn't. Practise first on a piece of white card which has been coated with gesso, blending one colour from the left and the other from the right, until you can get a smooth transition from one colour

to the other. Next, build up the colour on the wings, tail, back and rump with thin washes of mix D.

The bill is a dark brown, almost straight Burnt Umber, with a little Napthol Light Red blended in at the base. When you have finished the blending, apply several coats of matt medium over the whole bill.

For the legs, apply one wash of matt medium with the barest hint of Napthol Light Red in it, which will give it a pink glow. Follow this with several washes of matt medium with a little Carbon Black added, which will give a translucent, light gray leg with an underlying hint of pink. Apply several more coats to the claws to make them a darker, mid-gray.

Fig 11.40 The carving has been painted with the gesso base coat, and the various colour areas planned.

Fig 11.41 Painting is almost complete, with just final detailing and tidying up to do.

Fig 11.42 Three views of the completely painted bird.

FINISHING AND ASSEMBLY

To finish, apply several thin coats of matt medium and Carbon Black to the quills with a fine, liner brush. The carving is now ready for a critical appraisal. After painting, I like to leave the carving where I can see it, for a week or so if possible, and then go back and make any minor adjustments that I think are needed. It is surprising, there is always something, no matter how careful you were in the first place.

Colours can be adjusted on the bird by applying thin washes of another colour; Ultramarine, for example, will darken the browns, and when dried the change will not be blue, but a quite subtle darkening and cooling of the colour, if the wash was thin enough.

It now remains only to try the bird in place on the rock. Keep the colour mixes and live with the carving for a few days until you are sure that you are happy with the painting before finally gluing it in place with rapid epoxy glue.

Fig 11.43 A more traditional style of mounting for a similar carving; the base is turned in a piece of beautifully figured burr elm.

CHAPTER 12
GREEN WOODPECKER

THE SUBJECT

The largest of the three British wood-peckers, the green woodpecker (*Picus viridis*), with its unusual 'laughing' call, is one of the more colourful and exotic of our native species. It is also, usually, the only British woodpecker that you will see on the ground, hunting for ants and other insects. There are a few birds resident in some woodland quite near where I live, and while I don't normally see any around the village, the day after starting this project I spotted the familiar dipping flight and flash of green as one left the churchyard.

Woodpeckers are a slightly more difficult bird to mount on a branch than most; their tail is used like the third leg of a tripod, to give stability to the bird when it attacks a tree with its massive bill, and this pushes the tail feathers hard against the tree, causing the tips to bend. This gives an added challenge to the second project, because it means the tail has to be very accurately carved to fit the branch you are using. The tail feathers have extremely thick quills, and are usually heavily abraded at the tips — caused by the bird sitting back on them. The feet have two toes pointing forward and two pointing back to give maximum grip against forces in either direction. These, coupled with the strong tail, give the bird the maximum possible stability.

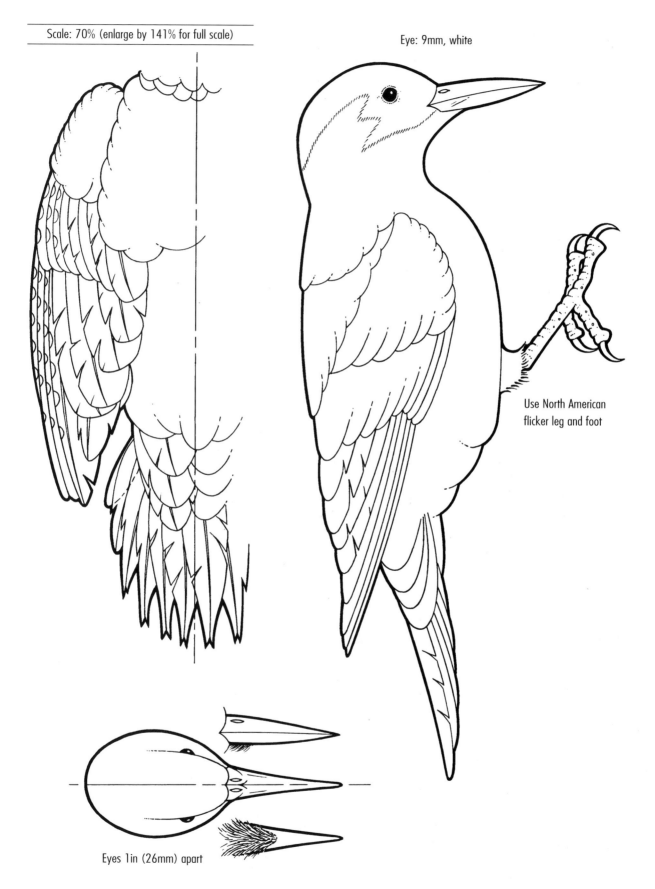

Scale: 70% (enlarge by 141% for full scale)

Eye: 9mm, white

Use North American
flicker leg and foot

Eyes 1in (26mm) apart

Fig 12.1 Green woodpecker (*Picus viridis*).

THE BASIC CONCEPT AND DESIGN

Although they can be found on the ground, the most usual place for a woodpecker is up a tree, so this is where I put it. This piece was actually a commission, so it had to be particularly well planned from the outset, before I could make any promises to the client about price and time scale. I had to ascertain whether or not I had a suitable mounting branch, collect sufficient information to do the drawing, carving and painting, and produce some rough sketches of my ideas for approval.

I have a shed full of 'interesting bits of wood' which I collect whenever I am out walking the dog. You can often look at a piece of branch and immediately visualize a certain species of bird sitting there, but it is slightly more difficult, when the species is already decided, to find the piece of branch that is just right. This is why I never carve a bird and then find 'a bit of wood' to put it on, as it is quite likely that they would look uncomfortable together, unless I was very lucky. The green woodpecker is a fairly large bird and I didn't want it to dwarf the branch it was mounted on, though I didn't want a massive tree trunk either.

After an hour of searching, I found, at the bottom of the pile, a nicely shaped, curved branch, about two feet long and tapering to the tip. I searched my files for suitable pictures and found disappointingly few for such a photogenic bird (though as could be predicted, I have found plenty of good photographs since completing the carving), so I rang around a few contacts to see what I could come up with. I finally borrowed some good close-up slides of a woodpecker being held in the hand, from the warden of the nature reserve on Rutland Water. I had some C. F. Tunnicliffe sketches in a book, and the local museum supplied a rather ragged old specimen from its stores, and a study skin of an immature bird, so I was ready to get started.

As soon as I had determined the profile shape of the bird, I made up a cardboard cut-out to try on the branch, which was, by now, screwed to a temporary wooden base, to check the relative sizes and shapes of bird and branch, and make sure they worked. I made the cardboard bird with a hinged tail section so that I could get the relationship between the body, tail and branch correct, before finalizing the pattern. When the cardboard tail was correctly adjusted and stapled in place, I returned to the drawing board.

Whilst I continued to work on the drawings, I sent sketches of the arrangement to the client for approval. When a new drawing is completed, I like to try it out very quickly to find out if the overall shape and bulk of the bird works. I am not bothered about small details, but only what the bird-watchers call the Jizz, the overall impression. Sometimes I make a Plasticine model, especially if the carving has to have a complex pose, mirroring the shape of the mount perhaps. Simple poses often get bandsawn out and quickly carved from a lump of jelutong, using a large Karbide Kutzall; in half an hour I will know whether the drawing is near enough or not and if it is, the roughed-out bird can be finished as a stylized version at a later date. (This trial version must have worked out okay, as it was stolen from a gallery a little while after I'd finished it!)

THE BLANK

Once I was happy with the overall effect, I prepared card patterns for marking out the timber block prior to bandsawing. (*See* Maquettes in Chapter 5, on page 42.) I cut the blank in tupelo, my favourite timber, allowing a minimum of 1–1 1/4in (25–32mm) of tail thickness for carving – much more than you would normally allow. (*See* Chapter 6.) Once you have cut out the blank, hold it against the branch and mark the position and direction of the legs in pencil. Drill the blank and the branch to take the leg wires, and attach the legs to the blank temporarily, with a spot of adhesive from a hot melt glue gun. Two pieces of wire of the correct length are all that are

needed to make wire legs, or you could use cast metal legs of the North American flicker, whose dimensions are very close to the green woodpecker. Fit the blank to the branch temporarily, to see which areas need to be carved away, and mount the branch on a board, again, temporarily.

FITTING THE TAIL TO THE BRANCH

With the blank held in place on the branch, slip carbon paper between the branch and tail, with the carbon surface facing the cut-out. Rock the blank gently over the carbon paper to mark where they touch, then remove the blank from the branch. Where the tail block touched the branch, there should be a deposit of carbon; shave this away, and try the blank on the branch again. Repeat this procedure as many times as

necessary to get a good close fit between the underside of the tail block and the branch. It is often possible to make minor adjustments to the branch by carving or filling, especially if it has no bark, but these alterations are difficult to hide if the branch is not being painted. Once the underside of the tail has been fitted to the branch, drill both the branch and the tail to take a small metal rod – together with the legs, this will give a firm, three point fixing to the finished carving.

The portion of the underside of the tail which has been fitted to the branch, will accommodate the curved tip of the tail where it is pushed against the tree. Draw the line of the finished tail on the edge of the tail block, which is still over-thick, and remove some of the waste to give the same sort of thickness you would normally allow the tail – approximately ½in (13mm).

Fig 12.2 The bandsawn blank is temporarily fitted to the branch to see what areas need to be carved away.

Fig 12.3 The underside of the tail is carved away to fit the surface of the branch: several fittings are needed before a perfect fit is achieved.

INITIAL HEAD SHAPING

The next step is to correct the head shape on the blank. Because the bird is being carved from one piece of tupelo, the original sawn profile leaves the head looking straight forward. Redraw the profile with the head turned 20–30°, to give a more animated pose, and use a coping saw to remove the initial waste from the redrawn head. You will see that it has the usual two high and two low quadrants on the top of the head, distorting the overall shape. (*See* the Big Dipper sequence in Figs 6.13–6.18). This has to be corrected before you do any further work; if you cannot get the head shape right before you have removed too much timber, the blank will have to be scrapped, or the head cut off and a new one dowelled and glued in place. I prefer to carve the whole bird from one piece of timber wherever possible, as it gives more integrity to the carving, and also because there are no glue lines to hide – an important advantage.

Remove the two high corners from the head first (these lie at right angles to the original centre-line), and draw the new centre-line on the head before removing any more timber. The head shape can now be corrected as follows:

1 Looking down the new bill line, hold the bird so that you can just see the front of the crown area; you will see a 'horizon' where one side will be high and one low. Remove some timber from the high side, so that the profile looks fairly even on both sides of the centre-line. Only remove wood as far as the horizon.

2 Still looking down the centre-line, hold the blank so that a new horizon can be seen a little behind the first, and remove some more wood to even up the shape either side of the centre-line. Work from the front to the back of the head, evening up the shape as you go, slowly altering how you hold the bird to reveal a new horizon.

3 Carry out the same procedure, this time working from the back of the head to the front.

The horizons are imaginary lines at right angles to the centre-line, and approximately ¼–⅜in (6–10mm) apart. You can actually draw them on the head if you wish, as I did with the dipper, in the previous chapter. The top of the head should now be even, and attention can be turned to the top profile of the head, drawing it accurately onto the new surface. Trim the head to the maximum width, which is usually the dimension at the centre of the cheeks, just below and behind the eye. The chin area under the bill also needs correcting. To do this, remove material from under the bill, on the side the head is turned to. This will make the throat area lie at right angles to the new centre-line. Once the head is fully shaped, assess it critically to make sure that it has not ended up too small, before turning your attention to the rest of the body.

INITIAL BODY SHAPING

I first remove the sharp corners, and generally round up the blank to take the 'blockiness' away. This gives it a more rounded, bird-like shape and leaves marking out easier. Avoid rounding the areas that are to become the lower edges and tips of the wings or the tail, as material might be removed which will be needed later. The rounding is done mainly in the breast, back and belly areas. It can be done with a knife, a coarse Karbide Kutzall, a hard sanding drum – whatever suits your temperament and the contents of your tool kit.

Draw on the bottom edge of the wing, then define and relieve this with a cylindrical carbide cutter, and re-round the belly. Remove the area between the leg tufts so that the line of the belly can run through to the tail coverts. Round the upper tail covert area, under the wings, using a finger-shaped carbide cutter – again, avoid removing the areas which will be needed for the tail feathers.

Once the overall body shape has been established, sand the bird smooth so that the feather groups can be clearly and accurately marked out. I used a soft sander in the flexi-drive for this, and finished off by hand. Use only 80 grit, cloth-backed abrasive, as the idea is to smooth out carving marks and get rid of deep scratches, and not to achieve a glass-like finish at this stage.

INITIAL APPRAISAL

Examine the carving critically again, and try it back on the branch. This is the make or break point – if it doesn't look right now, finishing the beak and carving feathers all over it is not going to improve matters. This is the last real opportunity to correct any major faults in the shape or size before the

time-consuming detail carving and texturing is carried out. If I couldn't correct any defects at this stage, only a few hours into a carving, I would scrap it rather than waste all the time that the detail work entails. If you do need to take the drastic step of throwing away your first attempt, it is most important to note where material needs to be added, or the shape changed, and then to alter the pattern so that you don't just repeat the same mistakes over again. If you didn't manage to get the head shape correct until it was only sparrow sized, then exaggerate it on the pattern – it is much easier to take a little off all over, once you have got the profile corrected. This applies to commercial patterns as well as the ones you create yourself; allow extra material in areas where you think you may have problems establishing the correct shape.

Fig 12.4 The body is carved and sanded to the general overall shape. . .

Fig 12.5 . . . and the feather groups are marked out for carving.

REFINING THE HEAD

Improve the head shape further, by drawing in the bill and bringing it nearer to size, using a straight, tapered ruby carver, and form the beginnings of the eye groove and cheeks with a ball-shaped ruby carver. As the bill is so massive, there is little fear of damaging it. Establish the eye position, and carefully drill the eye holes. (*See* Fixing the eye position in Chapter 11, on page 94; *see also* Chapter 9.) The head and bill are still not brought down to final dimensions at this stage, but left just a little over-size to allow for detailing and feather carving. A lot of care is needed in the carving of the head, as it is the focal point of the carving, and the success of the final piece depends as much on this area as it does on all the rest of the carving put together.

FEATHER CLUMPS AND GROUPS

Mark out the general feather groups over the smooth wing surface and then carve and sand them, to add volume and shape to the wing. Similarly, draw feather groups all over the rest of the body, to break up the smooth egg-like body shape into coherent clumps of feathers. (*See* Feather carving in Chapter 11, on page 90; *see also* Chapter 7.) Particular attention must be paid to the head, upper breast, and cape areas, as the head is the main point of focus for the eye when viewing the finished carving.

Thin the tail further and establish the upper and lower tail coverts. (*See* Wings and tail in Chapter 11, on page 89.) The end of the tail should now look as if it were bent hard against the branch, as it would be in real life when supporting the weight of the woodpecker.

Having marked out all the lumps and clumps of feathers, outline them with a ball-shaped cutter, and then round them over. I used ruby carvers; a long, tapered one for working on the bill, and two sizes of ball-shaped cutter ¼ and ⅜in (6 and 10mm), for the feather clumps. They need outlining

rather more deeply than you would at first expect, because the bird is then thoroughly sanded to blend these lumps into the overall body shape. The transitions from one bump to the next should be smooth with no sign of a 'ditch' between them, but rather, undulations in the surface, which give a soft look to the finished work.

When using the ball cutter, it is always important that the cutter moves across the surface in the same direction as the flow of the feathers or the barbs of the individual feather. This way, any small undulations left by the cutter will blend in and add to the overall texture and softness; this is particularly important on the head where individual feathers will not actually be carved. You need to identify feather clumps when drawing the individual feathers, so as I sand up each feather clump, I outline it in pencil again to help with this identification – when the sanding is finished, the effect can be so subtle as to make the identification of individual clumps difficult. You may find it advantageous to quickly sketch all the feathers over the surface of the bird first, to help identify potential feather clumps before carving them. If so, work on a small area at a time and redraw the feather outlines as soon as you finish sanding each small section, so that you end up with the original planned arrangement.

Fig 12.6 The beak is partially carved, and the feather groups of the head are marked on.

Fig 12.7 Marking
out the wings . . .

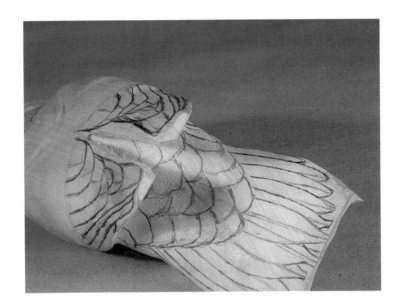

Fig 12.8 . . . the
upper tail coverts . . .

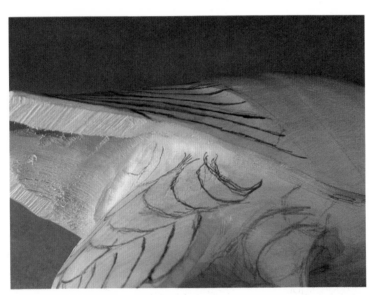

Fig 12.9 . . . and
the individual tail
feathers.

HARD-EDGED FEATHERS

I always start by carving the hard-edged feathers that form the wings and the tail, as they are overlapped by soft feather areas. These feathers have well-defined shapes and do not blend into each other in the same way as the soft body feathers. They have to be drawn in very carefully, with constant reference to the drawing. I carve the wing and tail feathers individually, constantly checking the shape and relative positions of the feathers in each group. If any large breaks or splits are to be carved in these feathers, they need to be drawn in at this stage, to allow for the change in edge contour that occurs with a large feather split. I also draw in the first row of soft feathers where they overlap the hard-edged ones. This allows for feather splits and overlaps to be planned there, giving a more subtle transition from one type of feather to the other.

Before the upper surface of the wings can be carved, the underside needs thinning and shaping. A lot of waste was left here when the pattern was bandsawn, and if you try to remove it after carving the top surface, the work may be damaged. In

addition to removing wood from the underside of the wings, a smooth, curved surface from the tail area up onto the back must also be created at this stage. Use a long, finger-shaped Karbide Kutzall, followed by a long-bladed knife, a gouge, and finally sandpaper, to get a good smooth surface on which to draw the feathers.

Reduce the wings to approximately ¼in (6mm) thick at the edges, but leave the centre thicker to give them more strength. Outline the wing and tail feathers and rough them out with a small, cylindrical diamond cutter which has a smooth, 'safe' end.

Fig 12.10 The wing and tail feathers are now individually carved, with the tips of the tail curved up where they press against the branch; these are the hard-edged feathers.

Fig 12.11 Tail and wing areas have now been roughly carved . . .

Fig 12.12 . . . and the feathers are marked out on the rest of the body.

SOFT FEATHER AREAS

Attention now turns back to the soft feather areas. Unlike the dipper, which had an overall texture, this carving has more individual feathers, which should now be drawn over the previously carved lumpy feather groups. This is where the pencil lines reminding you of where the groups are actually meant to be come in useful. Outline and shape the individual feathers with a suitably sized, ball-shaped ruby carver. The outlining needs to be fairly deep, as by the time the back of each feather is relieved towards its overlapping feather, and the surface has been shaped like a convex shell, you will be back to an almost smooth surface if you didn't go deep enough to start with! The aim is to give a slightly exaggerated, puffed up look to each feather, which will give a soft appearance on the finished carving. The effect should not be too even though – variation in the depth of the feather carving in different areas will add to the natural soft effect.

When all the soft feathers have been relieved and shaped, sand them using a small, split mandrel with sanding cloth wrapped round it, and then finish off by hand. Sand each individual feather carefully, so that its shape is retained. A very smooth finish is required before texturing; damp the wood slightly, with methylated spirit or warm water, to raise the grain before a final sanding with 400 or 600 grit paper when it dries. I usually finish off with a Scotchbrite pad mounted on an arbor, instead of the fine wet-and-dry paper. The smoother the surface achieved, the less likely it is for wood fibres to be torn up from the carving during texturing, and mar the effect. The finished surface should consist of soft feather-like shapes which flow into each other in all directions, with no trace of a hard line surrounding any soft feather, only an indistinguishable transition from one to another.

After sanding, all the feathers need to be drawn in lightly again, prior to texturing. This is not always that easy to do if you have managed to get the transition areas really

soft. Refer back to the study material if you are unsure about the feather layout, and make sure you are really happy with the pencilled feather layout before you start the texturing.

Fig 12.13 The soft feather areas are defined . . .

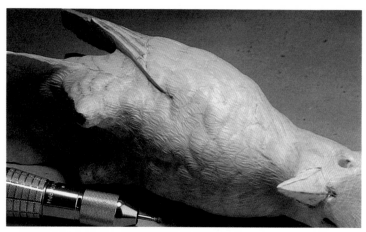

Fig 12.14 . . . and individually ground.

Fig 12.15 Small splits are sanded and burned in the hard-edged feathers before texturing.

ADDING FEATHER SPLITS

Carve the planned feather splits with a small knife, and soften the edges of the splits by sanding.

TEXTURING AND BURNING THE FEATHERS

INITIAL FEATHER TEXTURING

Give the feathers a base texture of shallow lines and ripples, with a small, round, abrasive stone about $\frac{1}{8}$in (3mm) in diameter; curved lines following the feather barbs can be sketched on the feather beforehand as a guide, but this is not really necessary. Quills are generally not noticeable on soft feather areas, as they are very fine and usually only the tip of the feather is seen, so the feather texturing can be done in a series of inwardly curved marks, with a change in direction mid-feather. Do not cover every single bit of the feathers with the base texture, but give some just a few strokes and cover others with an even set of lines – variation in the surface treatment is one key to a natural, soft look. Treat areas with no distinct

Fig 12.16 The initial feather texturing of the soft feather areas over the sides . . .

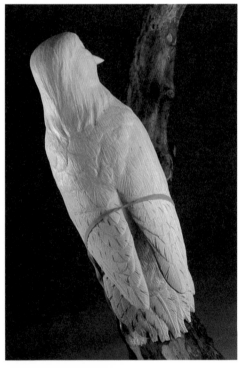

Fig 12.17 . . . and the top of the body is completed . . .

Fig 12.18 . . . leaving the hard-edged feathers under the tail area to complete, before all the hard-edged feathers are given a base texture.

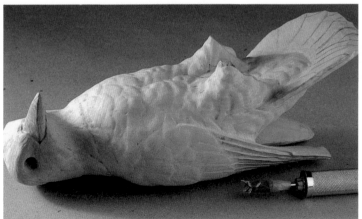

individual feathers to a texturing pattern, flowing over the surface in the way that the feathers would lie.

I often alternate work on different parts of the bird so that no area is completed and liable to damage too early in the carving process. Following this work on the soft feathers, I returned to the hard-edged feathers of the wing and tail.

Adjust the fit of the underside of the tail to the branch to as near perfect as possible – it will never be as close as if you carved tail and branch from one piece of timber, but with care it should be close. You can now shape and sand all these hard-edged feathers, imparting to them a curved top surface. Emery boards (used for nail manicures) are quite useful here, or alternatively, pieces cut from fine Sandvik Sandplate could be used. Use the pyrograph to clean up any awkward corners and to burnish off any wood fibres. If a large area of an individual hard-edged feather is showing, I will first use a large, ball-shaped abrasive stone, $\frac{3}{8}$ or $\frac{1}{2}$in (10 or 13mm), to form ripples in the surface and in the exposed outer edge of the feather. This is just a more extreme version of the initial surface texture, but it adds more realism and interest to the feather.

FORMING QUILLS IN HARD-EDGED FEATHERS

Outline the quills with a safe-ended, cylindrical, diamond cutter, before tidying them up with the pyrograph, held at a shallow angle to the feather surface. Finally, sand the individual quills with very fine abrasive cloth to round them over. The tail quills are very heavy, $\frac{1}{16}$in (2mm) or more in diameter, and only taper very slightly towards the tip so that they can support the weight of the bird. The feather tips, continually rubbed against the bark, wear away very quickly and become quite shabby, but I would normally carve the bird in its prime – usually with breeding plumage.

After carving the quills, form a base texture on the feathers with a small, fine, ball-shaped, abrasive stone, as was used on the soft feather areas, then thoroughly

texture the hard-edged feathers with a small, inverted, cone-shaped, fine white abrasive stone. Be careful not to nick the shaft with the stone, as nicks are easily seen and very difficult to disguise. Finally, texture the feathers using a pyrograph with a well-honed tip, running at a medium heat so that the lines can be set very close to each other. It is important to keep them close and to thoroughly cover the entire feather surface. Curve the burn lines and start them up against the quill so that they cover any areas left bare by the texturing stones. Again, be very careful not to nick the quill with the pyrograph.

Variation in the burnt texture can be achieved by starting the burn line slowly, speeding up along the line, and flicking off at the end. This gives a deeper, darker burn at the quill and a lighter, shallower burn at the edge. I use a headband magnifier when doing the close burning; it is a great help, and if it looks good through the magnifier, then it will look even better when viewed without.

You can also burn each half of the feather in two stages, to give a harder, more defined edge and a softer looking centre. Burn from the quill outwards, flicking off the pen as you get towards the centre of the feather area, then do the reverse, starting at the feather edge and burning inwards. This method also allows you to get the soft S shape of the feather barbs rather than the simple curve, so it is useful on larger feathers where the effect can be seen properly.

REFINING AND TIDYING UP

Undercutting the edges of some feathers with the pyrograph will give more separation between overlapping feathers, and one or two deeper, heavier burn lines can be added to simulate small splits. The pyrograph can also be used to get some separation at the feather tips, which couldn't be readily achieved with normal tools. In fact, it is a very useful carving tool for adding and tidying up fine details.

After burning is complete, brush the burnt areas with an old toothbrush to

remove the carbon – brush with the lines, not across them, to prevent damage. With the carbon removed, examine the feathers for missed lines or large gaps between lines, and burn any extra lines to fill them in.

With the hard-edged feathers complete, finish texturing the soft feather areas with a small, cylindrical, fine white stone. Start from the back and work forward so that the texturing overlaps in the same way as the feathers. Make sure that the whole surface is completely textured, but don't texture the front of the head until the bill is finished.

BACK TO THE HEAD

FINISHING THE BILL

Carve and sand the bill to its final dimensions, and use the pyrograph to burn on the details and clean up the edge where it meets the feather-line. Soak the finished bill tip with thin superglue to toughen it. (*See* Finishing the bill in Chapter 11, on page 95.)

FITTING THE EYES

Test the fit of the glass eyes: they need to be a loose fit in the eye holes so that they don't jam when being fitted. If the fit is alright,

soften the eye hole edge by sanding it with a roll of abrasive before the texturing of the front of the head is completed.

I used museum quality taxidermy, aspheric glass eyes with a white iris, and seated them in a bed of Milliput epoxy putty. They can be positioned in the socket with the eraser end of a pencil. The back face of the eye should remain in the same

Fig 12.19 The hard-edged feathers are given their final texture on the wings . . .

Fig 12.20 . . . and on the tail, using the pyrograph.

Fig 12.21 The eyes are fitted, and the carving is given a final try on the branch before painting. The branch has now been fitted to a turned burr elm base.

vertical axis as the head, and the front of the eye should tilt in to look forwards. (*See* Eyes in Chapter 11, on page 101; *see also* Chapter 9.) It is important that the eyes are set to the correct depth; too deep and they will end up undersized and lost in the eyelid, too shallow and they will look like organ stops. Epoxy putty gives plenty of working time, so the eye position can be adjusted until you are completely happy with the result.

FORMING THE EYE RINGS

Form the eye rings from two small, thin rolls of DuroMend ribbon epoxy. Cut one of these to length, and lay it round the eye, adjusting it with old dental probes to give a nicely shaped pupil. Push the tools into Plasticine occasionally to keep them slightly oiled, so that the putty doesn't stick. Squash a very small portion of the outer edge of the epoxy ring with a pointed dental probe, and draw it out into the texturing around the eye. Repeat this all round the ring to fix it in place, before carefully smoothing the eye ring around the joint, and making any final adjustments to its shape. (*See* Eye rings in Chapter 11, on page 102.)

To texture the eye ring, give the surface a knobbly texture by lightly pressing the end of a modified hypodermic needle onto the surface. (The end of a hypodermic needle is

oblique and needs to be stoned off square before use. The sizes used by veterinary surgeons, available at agricultural chemists, are the most useful; needles intended for humans are usually too fine.)

With the eyes now fitted, check the appearance of the bird on the branch once more, before starting to paint the carving.

PAINTING

CLEANING AND SEALING

Carefully brush the fully textured bird with an old toothbrush, to remove most of the dust and debris, before brushing again with a small, soft, nylon rotary brush, run at slow speed, to really clean out the depths of the texturing. All brushing must be done with the direction of the texturing, not across it. This will also detach some of the small wood fibres which will almost certainly be lurking amongst the texturing lines.

Mount the carving on a 'painting stick'; as the legs have not yet been glued in place, the screw can be inserted in one of the leg holes without damage. The painting sticks I use are various sized pieces of dowel, with a woodscrew glued in the end. Drill a few holes in a large block of wood, to use as a stand when you need to put the carving

Fig 12.22 The bird is screwed to a painting stick through one leg hole, for ease of handling.

Fig 12.23 It is then given undercoats of gesso, before the red and black areas are added to the head.

aside. (This method works well for larger birds on legs, but for smaller birds I fix the legs temporarily in wooden blocks.)

Check the carving carefully for any bits that have been missed, before sealing it with two or three coats of thinned cellulose sanding sealer (1 part sealer to 1 part thinner). Brush this onto the carving in thin coats, following the lines of texturing, and avoiding runs and puddles, to stop any build-up hiding the surface detail.

When the sealer has thoroughly dried (about 15 mins), brush out the texturing with a rotary brush again, but this time use a stiffer, natural bristle one. The sealer will have hardened the texturing, giving it more protection from the brush, and at the same time, it will have stiffened any remaining wood fibres lurking down in the texture lines. These will now usually break away during the final brushing, leaving clean, smooth texturing. You always need to be careful, when using any brush, to brush along the texturing lines and not across them, even after sealing.

APPLYING THE UNDERCOAT

Now that the carving is ready for painting, apply an undercoat of white acrylic gesso, tinted to the pale green base colour of the

---

COLOUR MIXES

MIX A

Gesso undercoat

White acrylic gesso plus very small amounts of Carbon Black, Hooker's Green (Rowney Cryla), and Opaque Oxide of Chromium (Rowney Cryla)

MIX B

Grayish green crown and black cheek markings

1 part Burnt Sienna to 1 part Ultramarine (Rowney Cryla)

MIX C

Red cheek patches

Washes of Napthol Light Red over an undercoat of Iridescent Silver (Liquitex)

MIX D

Red feather edges on crown

1 part Napthol Light Red to 1 part Cadmium Red (Rowney Cryla)

MIX E

General red brush on crown

1 part Cadmium Red (Rowney Cryla) to 1 part matt medium plus a little Iridescent Silver (Liquitex)

MIX F

Bill tip

Equal amounts of Burnt Umber and Burnt Sienna

MIX F2

Glaze for bill

Mix F plus a little matt medium (paint sample not shown)

MIX G

Dirty green on back

Yellow Oxide plus a little Hooker's Green (Rowney Cryla) plus Carbon Black

MIX H

Brown on legs

Equal amounts of Burnt Umber and Raw Umber plus Carbon Black

MIXING TIP
Mix plenty of paint for all the colours, and store the excess in 35mm film containers until required.

bird (mix A). Several coats are required, with the mix thinned to a single cream consistency, and brushed on with a fairly stiff hog bristle brush, of the type used for oil painting. Brush the paint on, following the direction of the texturing so that when it dries, no brush strokes will be left running across texture lines instead of along them. The stiff brush forces the paint down into the texturing grooves to give complete coverage. Allow the undercoat to dry naturally for the first couple of coats: if a hairdryer is used to speed the drying up, as it is later in the painting, bubbles of gesso dry in the texturing and then break, leaving pinholes which are almost impossible to paint over at a later stage. Make sure that the colour you mix is not too dark, as it is easier to darken it with a further wash of colour, than it is to lighten it again.

The colour changes in plumage are much more subtle on the green woodpecker than the dipper, so it is not possible to be very specific about how the paints are mixed and used. Painting with acrylic washes, which are basically transparent, enables the colour to be built up to different values. Putting on a considerably darker (not thicker) wash, will have only a slight effect on the overall colour of the area being worked on, so subtle variations in hue can be achieved. If a good rendering of the subtle variations of the plumage is to be achieved, good reference material and some practise on card is necessary before starting on the bird.

APPLYING THE COLOURS

Draw in the coloured markings of the head with a white watercolour pencil. I often use these when painting, as if you paint over them, they are combined with the acrylic paint, and because of the minute amount of pigment in a fine line, are lost in the first coat. If there are any remaining pencil marks after painting they can be easily removed by brushing with clean water.

Paint the grayish green crown and black cheek markings with thin washes of mix B, until the correct depth of colour has been built up in each area.

For the red cheek patches, apply an undercoat of Iridescent Silver (Liquitex), and then paint over this with washes of Napthol Light Red (mix C). The red crown actually consists of gray feathers with red edges, so next, edge the feathers on the gray crown with mix D, and then use a liner brush to pull thin lines of this colour through the feather edges. Once you have done this, apply a thin wash of Carbon Black, and finally, dry brush over it with mix E. This complex effect has to be painted in a rather intuitive manner to get the desired effect, however, you could compromise and dry brush the red mix straight over the gray.

Apply an undercoat of white gesso to the bill, then add Yellow Oxide to the sides, base and top, and wet blend this into the other white areas. Darken the tip of the bill with mix F, wet blended. (*See* Blending in Chapter 10, on page 77.) Now paint the whole bill with several coats of mix F2, until the required overall tone is achieved. Finish the bill with several coats of matt medium to build up a waxy, nail-like appearance.

Darken the back with mix G, wet blended to the lighter coloured base areas. When satisfied with the depth of colour, apply a very thin wash of mix G over the base green, everywhere but the cheeks.

Fig 12.24 After the head is completed, green washes are applied to the body to build up the colour.

Fig 12.25 The white markings on the primaries are painted, and the rest of the primary feathers are darkened.

To colour the primary feathers, wet blend the white markings onto the edges before darkening the feathers with several washes of Payne's Gray (Rowney Cryla), followed by an overall wash of Raw Umber (Liquitex).

Use washes of Raw Umber to darken the tail and apply the markings. When this has been done, darken the markings from the tips towards the base, with washes of Payne's Gray. Apply several coats of matt medium to the quills with a liner brush, to give them a waxy appearance.

FINISHING AND ASSEMBLY

Remove the carving from the painting stick and glue the legs and tail peg into position, on the body only, using epoxy glue. Use elastic bands to hold the carving in place on the branch until the glue has set. This ensures that the legs are correctly positioned when it is finally fixed in place.

Blend the leg tufts to the leg, where they join, using two small rings of DuroMend ribbon epoxy putty. Texture the putty with dental tools, oiled in a block of Plasticine to prevent them sticking to the epoxy.

When the putty is dry, apply an undercoat of white gesso to the legs, and then apply several washes of mix H, being careful not to make them too dark. Follow this with

a thin wash of white gesso, and finally, a very thin wash of Carbon Black. Darken the claws with Burnt Umber and wet blend the tips with Carbon Black, before giving them several coats of matt medium.

I used turned and polished burr elm for the base, and screwed the branch to this, gluing it as well for extra strength. I then covered the top of the base, around the branch, with a car body filler, and textured this with a brush to look like soil. To give it the natural colours of soil and algae, I painted the filler with a mixture of browns and greens. I used earth colours – umbers, siennas, and oxides – straight from the tube onto a dampened surface, so that they spread and blended.

When the paint had dried, I glued the carving in place, firmly located by the legs and the stainless steel pin inserted in the tail.

Fig 12.26 The legs are glued in place and painted before the completed bird is finally attached to the branch.

Fig 12.27 The finished project can be seen here from all angles.

CHAPTER 13

COMMON TERN

THE SUBJECT

The inspiration for this carving was a bird-watching trip to the National Trust-owned Farne Islands, off the wild Northumbrian coast in the north of England. In spring, the islands are a bird-watcher's paradise, with hardly a square yard of nesting space unoccupied by one or other of their breeding species. There are four breeding species of terns, plus kittiwakes, fulmars, puffins, guillemots, cormorants, shags and eiders in profusion, and so near that you could take photographs with your grannie's box Brownie! In fact, too near at times — you need a hat to protect yourself from the arctic tern's courageous dive-bombing attacks: that beak is as sharp as it looks! It is a truly magical place, and with the memory

of the tern's woodpecker attacks on my thinning pate still fresh, I went home to commence work.

Unfortunately, this project hit several snags along the way. Specifically, the museum could only supply a common tern skin, so, as it is a very close relative of the arctic tern, and I had seen common terns as well, I decided to carve that instead of the arctic tern, which had been my original choice. More generally, I felt that I wanted to carve and keep this project for myself and not sell it within a couple of weeks, so it kept getting shelved to make way for commissions and exhibitions, or writing projects, until this book gave me an ideal opportunity to revive it, so I dug out my drawings and gave them a dusting.

126

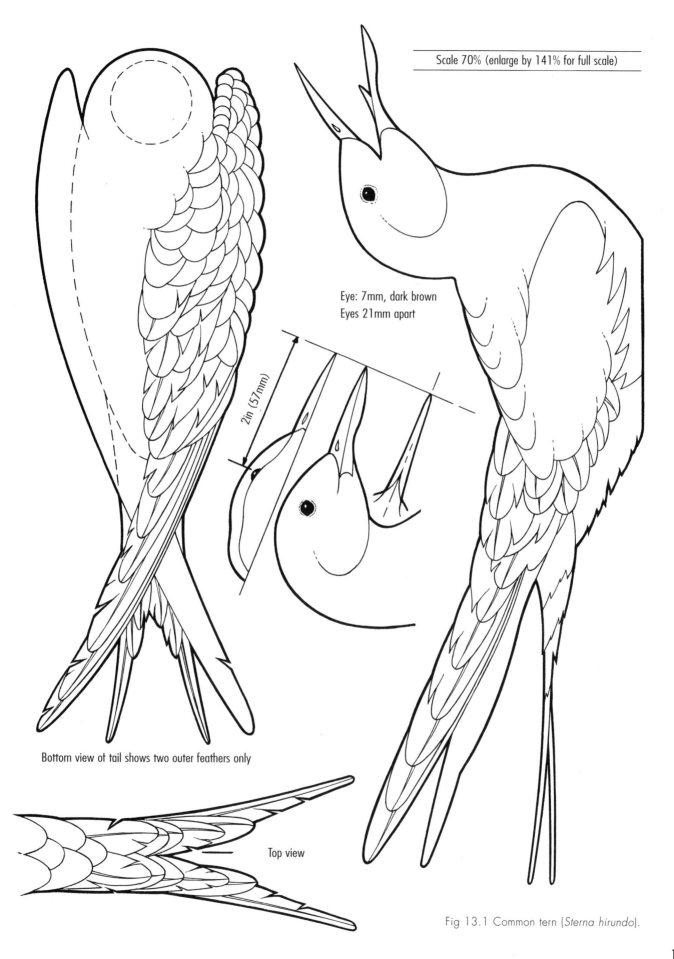

Scale 70% (enlarge by 141% for full scale)

Eye: 7mm, dark brown
Eyes 21mm apart

2in (57mm)

Bottom view ot tail shows two outer feathers only

Top view

Fig 13.1 Common tern (*Sterna hirundo*).

THE BASIC CONCEPT AND DESIGN

I had already decided to carve the bird calling from its nest scrape on a sandy beach; whilst most of the nests I photographed on the Farne Islands were obscured by undergrowth, I had seen quite a few photographs of terns at the nest. Even though I had never completed my original drawings, when I looked at them again after such a long break, I could see that I hadn't got the body shape quite right – the Jizz was wrong. Having just treated myself to the ultimate extravagance of a photocopier with enlarging and reduction facilities, I played around with portions of my drawing, some magazine photographs from my files, and a tracing pad, and within the hour had got what I wanted. As I live in 'the sticks', that would previously have taken me a couple of days, and several visits to the vicar. (He has an enlarging photocopier too!)

Because I was going to carve the tern at the nest, it would be flat-bottomed, rather like a decoy duck, and not necessarily require any base. However, I decided to set it on a turned base, with a small area of beach on the top. In the intervening period, between my original drawings and my return to the project, I had seen a picture of a really nice sculpture by Eldridge Arnold, which consisted of three least terns on a sand dune, facing into the wind. They were on a slope and had their tails higher than their heads. It was a very effective attitude, so I decided to incorporate that idea into the carving too. By banking up my nest scrape I could raise the wings and the tail up high.

THE BLANK

I prepared the cutting patterns from the drawings and a one-piece blank cut from tupelo. Tupelo will give the maximum strength to the wing tips and tail, which have the grain running the wrong way at the curved tips. This is a fairly challenging pattern to carve without using inserts, but it really only needs a little patience.

It would also be possible, however, to fit wing feather inserts to make carving and texturing of the upper rump, tail and under the wing easier, and to give maximum strength to the feathers. I think the best way to do this is to carve the bird in one piece, with the wings in place. The wings can then

Fig 13.2 The study skin and photographs used when updating the original drawing.

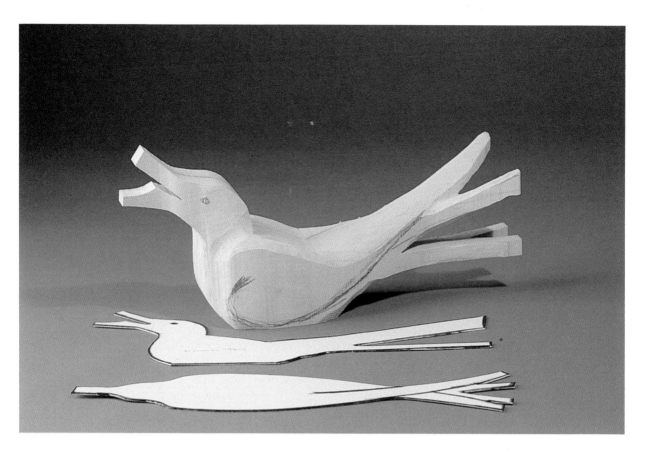

be cut off along the line of an overlapping feather group, and used as patterns for the new, carved wing inserts. With slots cut to receive the inserts in the area of the body from which the wings were removed, the surrounding area can be carved and textured easily. Carve the wing inserts to match the originals, and fit them in the slots, but do not glue them into place until after painting. This method helps ensure that the wing inserts flow correctly from the rest of the wing, and don't end up looking like they have just been stuck in!

THE BASE

The base is made in two parts; a turned wooden plinth rather like a platter, and a sub-base with the nest scrape. The sub-base will be carved and covered with shell gravel before being fitted into a turned recess in the top of the plinth.

Take a 9 x 9 x 2in (229 x 229 x 51mm) piece of jelutong, and slice it on the bandsaw to form two wedges. Tack them

together (I used glue and nails), and cut out an 8in (203mm) diameter circle. Turn the two wedges through 180°, and glue them back together to give a steeper wedge. Although I used this method to build up the thickness of the wedge, the timber I used not being of adequate thickness, this method does also save on timber usage. Carve a nest scrape into this base for the bird, and then round over and smooth the whole sub-base.

INITIAL BODY SHAPING

The first thing to do is to remove the extra material on the sides of the tail and between the wing tips, left by bandsawing to two profiles, and then to remove the extra material from the sides of the head. (*See* Chapter 6; *see also* Initial roughing out of the blank in Chapter 11, on page 88.) I left the head looking straight ahead, because the open bill would have caused difficulties if it had been turned 'in the block' like the dipper or the green woodpecker.

Fig 13.3 The patterns and bandsawn blank, after initial removal of waste from the tail and wings.

Now that the wing and tail shape can be seen properly, complete the initial rounding and modelling. (*See* Wings and tail in Chapter 11, on page89.) It is important that the line of the wing surface sweeps through from tip to wrist as a continuous plane. This is easy to do on the upper wing, but where it touches the lower one, it is easy to end up with a kink. For the initial shaping I used a large, cylindrical carbide rasp cutter, before coarse sanding to allow easier drawing in of detail. I sketched in the cape and breast feathers where they cover the wing, and pencilled in the wing feathers on the upper wing, before relieving all these areas with a small, cross-cut carbide burr.

Once you have established the upper wing surfaces, thin down the wing blocks and tidy up the area above the rump where they cross. Next, thin down the tail area, and give a slight curve to the tail, along its length. Establish the position of the lower tail coverts, and give the rump area some further shaping.

Fig 13.4 Cleaning up the wing cross-over using a thin, tungsten carbide file and flexible sanding strip.

Fig 13.5 The wing surface sanded and ready for marking out individual feathers; material has been left for the overlapping feather groups.

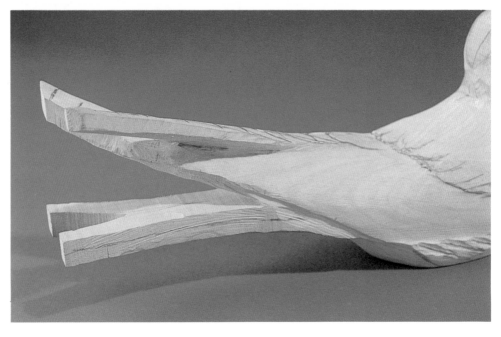

Fig 13.6 Individual wing feathers are marked out on the wing; note the overlapping cape feather group, which was later changed in shape.

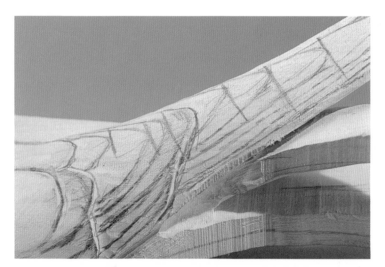

Fig 13.7 Feather tip positions are marked with a pencil line to make the drawing and subsequent re-drafting of feathers easier when marking out.

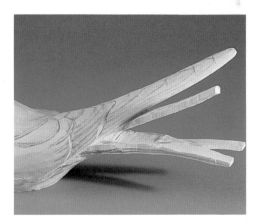

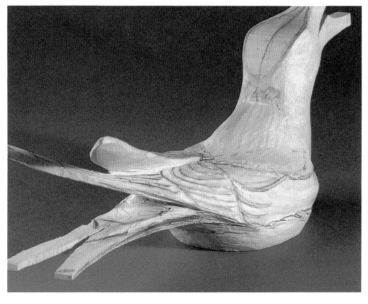

Fig 13.8 The tail is reduced in thickness, in readiness for marking out the individual feathers.

Fig 13.9 View of wings and tail showing preliminary carving.

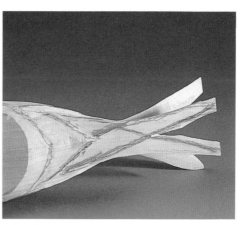

Fig 13.10 The main overlapping feather groups have been carved and highlighted in red.

Fig 13.11 Marking out the under-tail area.

Fig 13.12 Carving temporarily fitted on the sub-base to assess the success of the pose.

Fig 13.13 The lower tail covert area is carved, and the tail feathers shaped.

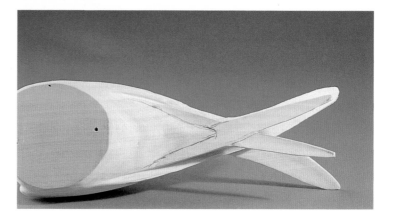

TURNING THE HEAD

Looking at the carving at this stage, I decided that it needed its head turned to give a bit more animation to the pose. I set about turning the head before I started on any further work, as this leaves more

material to work with when re-shaping the neck area. I cut the head off with a razor saw, which has such a narrow kerf (width of cut) that it doesn't require any extra material to be added to compensate. To do this, fix the body on a carving clamp, and remove the head carefully, cutting at a slight angle. The saw cut from a razor saw is fairly straight, but to make the glue line as narrow as possible, sand both glue faces. To get a really flat joint, use a piece of plate glass and a sheet of 320 grit wet-and-dry paper: place the plate glass on a table, lay the wet-and-dry paper over this, and draw the head across it. Great care must be taken not to round the joint when sanding, so I only sand in one direction, pulling the carving towards me whilst firmly holding it down. Coloured chalk can be rubbed on the glue face so that you can see when it is all sanded, and you can then check the face for flatness on the glass. By cutting off the head at a slight angle, you can make the head cock over to one side as it rotates on the neck, further adding to the animation of the piece.

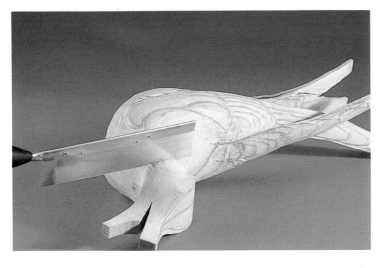

Fig 13.14 Removing the head with a razor saw.

Fig 13.15 Flattening the glue face with wet-and-dry paper on a sheet of glass.

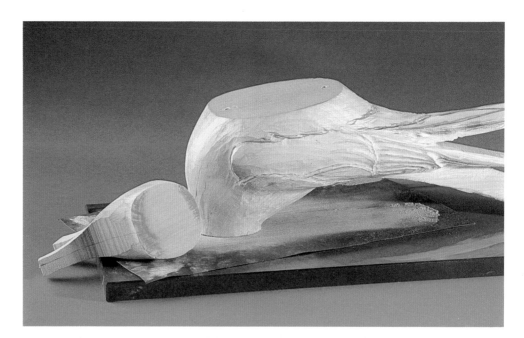

Fig 13.16 By chalking up the glue face you can see when it is really flat.

Fig 13.17 The head can now be turned to adjust the pose, and the position marked with the nail point.

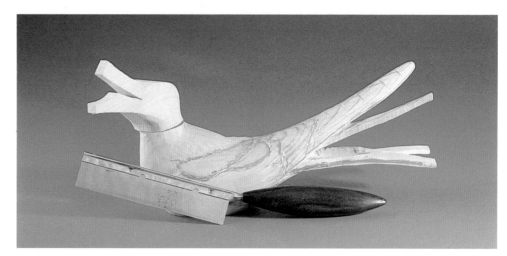

Fig 13.18 A dowel is used to reinforce the head/body joint, before gluing.

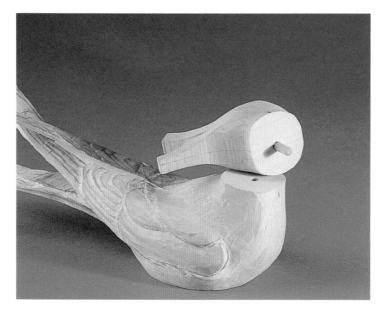

Mark the centre of the glue face on the body, and drill a $\frac{1}{32}$in (0.8mm) hole about $\frac{1}{2}$in (13mm) deep, then cut the head off a $\frac{3}{4}$in (19mm) panel pin, so that it will sit in the hole with the point sticking up about $\frac{1}{16}$in (1.6mm). Gently position the head, just rocking on the panel pin point. When the position is correct, push the head down firmly on the nail point, to mark the position. Now drill $\frac{1}{4}$in (6.35mm) holes at the positions marked on the head and body, just giving a loose fit for a $\frac{15}{64}$in (6mm) compressed beech dowel, allowing for a small margin of misalignment with the drilling. Check the fit of the faces once more, before gluing them together with Cascamite and its accelerator.

When the glue is dry, re-carve the neck joint and bring the head down to the thickness of the widest part, the cheeks, before removing the corners and rounding the crown. Draw the details onto the head in pencil, using callipers to transfer the critical dimensions, and locate the eye positions, aligning them with two awls, as for the dipper (*see* Fixing the eye position in Chapter 11, on page 94), before drilling a $\frac{1}{8}$in (3mm) hole for each. I used a pilot-drill for this. Now, partially form the eye grooves and cheeks using a $\frac{3}{8}$in (10mm) ball-shaped, fine Karbide Kutzall, and at last some idea of what the finished piece will look like emerges.

At this point I couldn't resist setting the carving on the nest and pouring shell gravel all over it to see what it was going to look like! It worked well, so I completed the nest scrape by painting it with PVA glue and then sprinkling it with shell gravel. Once you

have done this and the glue is dry, give the nest scrape two coats of thinned PVA glue to make sure all the gravel has bonded.

To make the plinth, turn and sand an 11 x 2in (280 x 51mm) disc of pitch pine to form a shallow, vase-shaped platter, with a recess in the top for the sub-base. After giving this plinth a final sanding, scorch it with a blowlamp, and then brush off the charring with a stiff brush, to bring out the pattern of the grain, and give it a weathered look. When this is done, paint the plinth with white acrylic gesso, and then tone this down with several colour washes, before giving it a final rub down with fine wire wool. If you would like a brown tint, use a wash of Raw Umber, and if you would like a silver finish, use a wash of Payne's Gray.

The assembly is left until later, as the carving will be fixed to the sub-base before both are then fixed to the turned plinth.

Fig 13.19 After gluing, the bird was set on the sub-base, and shell gravel heaped on this to get an idea of the finished composition.

WINGS AND TAIL

Because the open bill was going to be relatively delicate, I decided to leave all work on the head till last; the tail and wings can be carved to give as much thickness and strength as possible whilst maintaining the illusion of thinness and delicacy, but the beak and tongue do actually have to be thin.

Spend some time thinning the wings further and tidying them up where they cross, then do the same for the tail area. It is a fiddly area to work in, and I had to resort to using small files and the pyrograph to clean up in the confined space. If you can't get the far reaches cleaned up properly, you could use a little plastic wood, blended out with a brush and acetone thinner, to achieve a smooth, clean transition.

Fig 13.20 Outlining the hard-edged wing feathers with the pyrograph to form a stop cut.

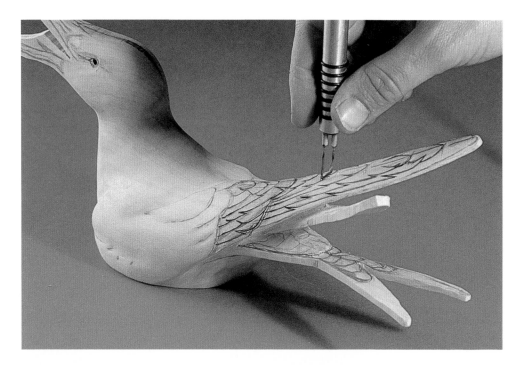

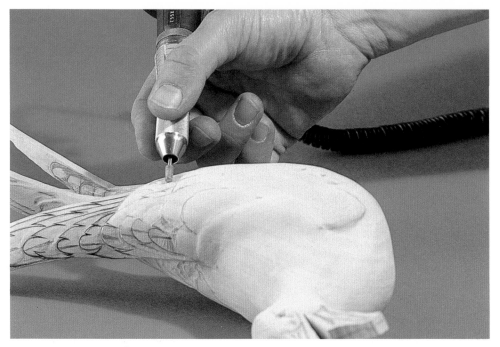

Fig 13.21 The feathers can be relieved with a knife, a small chisel, or, as here, a small, cylindrical cutter.

Fig 13.22 The wing and tail feathers have their overlapping feather groups redrawn before final shaping.

Fig 13.23 After all the individual feather groups have been shaped, they are sanded ready for texturing, and work on the head continues. Note that the sub-base has now been covered with shell gravel.

Draw out the individual feathers on the upper wing and tail surfaces, including the position of any feather splits. Outline the feathers with a stop cut, using the pyrograph, and then carve the individual feathers with a safe-ended, cylindrical diamond burr. Tidy the feather carving up, and then sand with an emery board. (*See* Feather carving in Chapter 11, on page 90; *see also* Chapter 7.)

With the top surface carved, draw a matching underside onto the wings and tail.

In this closed tail pose, the longest, outer tail feathers cross over to opposite sides of the tail, so the underside view only shows these two feathers.

The cape and breast feathers overlap onto the wing area. Draw these in next, then carve them with a ruby burr, and sand with rolled abrasive tape to soften the feather groups, making them 'melt' together. I carved several feather groups on the breast and neck, using a round burr, and then sanded to blend them in completely.

Fig 13.24 The study skin and reference notes are referred to when accurately marking out the head for carving the bill.

THE HEAD

To start work on the head, accurately measure and redraw the bill, and carefully widen the eye opening to $\frac{1}{4}$in (6mm). Shape and reduce the size of the bill in stages, until the correct measurements are almost achieved, leaving a margin for cleaning up and detailing.

Drill a hole through the open bill into the throat, and then open it up and shape with a $\frac{1}{4}$in (6mm) ball-shaped ruby carver. Use a pointed, bud-shaped ruby carver to hollow the upper and lower portions of the bill, then clean these up using fine riffler files. Again, I tidied up the deepest recess of the throat with a little plastic wood, smoothed with solvent and a brush. I used riffler files to obtain a flat-topped tongue, D-shaped in section.

Form a depression for the nostril in each side of the bill using a round diamond burr, then pierce and carve each nostril with a very fine, pointed diamond cutter. Tidy up the bill to feather intersection using the pyrograph, and sand the bill. Finally, soak the bill tips and the tongue with superglue to toughen them.

To complete the front of the head, carve it to match the now correctly sized bill,

being careful to get the nicely shaped and rounded cheek, which I think is one of the keys to satisfactory head shaping. (*See* Head in Chapter 11, on page 94.)

TEXTURING AND FEATHERS

The carving is now complete and ready to be sanded prior to texturing, although I can usually find one or two minor adjustments to be made at this stage. I aim to sand to a similar standard of finish as that required for

Fig 13.25 The head is given a final shaping and then sanded.

a polished hardwood carving, as this will texture cleaner, leaving fewer wood fibres to mar the work.

Before carving, redraw the quills and feather splits. Use a pointed, bud-shaped burr to carve the splits, and a safe-ended, cylindrical diamond burr to carve the quills. Carefully sand the quills and splits before lightly texturing the surface of the feathers with a fine grit, small round stone, following the line of the feather barbs. When all the hard-edged feathers have been textured like this, clean them up using Scotchbrite pads mounted on an arbor – this will leave the surface silky smooth.

Burn on the feather barbs, using the pyrograph set at a medium heat. The pyrograph can also be used to clean up corners where feathers overlap, and to add a small amount of undercut to feathers to define their shapes better. Always try to start burning in a less noticeable area, until you get into the rhythm and flow of burning the barbs. This way, any shaky, irregular lines will not be in the most prominent area of the carving.

When the burning is completed, draw on feather flow lines, covering the rest of the body, to act as guide lines for the actual texturing. (*See* Texturing soft feathers in Chapter 11, on page 97; *see also* Fig 10.2.) I used three different sizes of texturing stone, starting with the largest, about $\frac{3}{8}$in (10mm) diameter, and working down to the smallest, about $\frac{1}{8}$in (2.5mm) diameter. The surface was thoroughly textured so that no area was

Fig 13.26 The hard-edged feathers are textured and burnt.

Fig 13.27 Feather flow lines are pencilled over the body as a guide for texturing.

Fig 13.28 Three views of the fully-carved and textured bird, ready for fitting the eyes, and painting.

left untouched, and the pencilled guide lines helped to get the correct flow of the texturing over the body surface.

To de-fuzz the textured area I used the Scotchbrite pads which I had used earlier, and then carefully brushed out all the texturing and burning, using a soft rotary brush at slow speed, to remove any dust and debris. Soak the bill, tongue and vulnerable parts of the wing and tail with thin superglue to toughen them, before sealing the whole carving with two coats of thinned, cellulose sanding sealer.

EYES

Bed the 7mm dark brown eyes on epoxy putty, and adjust their positions until they look right. The eyes are quite small, so when making the eye rings it is important not to make them too thick, or the eye will be lost. Use ribbon epoxy to make the eye ring, and to texture it, use a flat-ended, hypodermic needle. (*See* Eyes in Chapter 11, on page 101; *see also* Chapter 9.) When you are satisfied with the eyes, set the carving aside for them to harden up.–

PAINTING

CLEANING AND SEALING

Give the entire carving a final brush over with a stiff rotary brush, following the lines of texturing, and dust it off with a soft brush to remove any debris. Apply a few coats of sealer before painting.

First, glue the carving to a scrap block of wood so that it can be handled more easily whilst painting. A flat-bottomed carving like this can be treated in the same way as a decoy duck, and have a temporary keel screwed or glued on. I used two or three spots of adhesive from a hot melt glue gun.

APPLYING THE BASE COLOUR

The base colour, mix A, is a warm, slightly brownish white. As with the other carvings, it needs to be thinned, and several coats applied to give an even base colour, without the paint filling in all the textured detail. In between coats I check for any bits of dried paint or dislodged debris and remove them with an old dental probe; this can also be used to burnish any odd fibres that have been left showing.

APPLYING THE COLOURS

Once the base coat is complete, paint the dark area on the head with mix B. I used

Fig 13.29 The entire bird has been given several coats of the brownish white base gesso colour, ready to start painting.

a gray watercolour pencil to lay out the area first. After this, paint the bill red, with mix C, and wet blend the bill tips, nostril and back of the throat with the warm black, mix B. (*See* Blending in Chapter 10, on page 77.)

To clean up the interface between the base coat and the black head, draw the base mix into the black area and vice versa, using

COLOUR MIXES

MIX A	MIX B	MIX C	MIX D	MIX D2
Gesso undercoat	Warm black on head	Red on bill	Gray on back	Darker shadows on back
1 part Raw Umber (Liquitex) to 20 parts white gesso	2 parts Burnt Umber to 1 part Ultramarine (Rowney Cryla)	1 part Norwegian Orange to 1 part Napthol Red Light	10 parts white gesso to 10 parts Neutral Gray, value 5 (Liquitex) to 1 part Carbon Black	Mix D plus a little more Carbon Black

MIXING TIP Mix plenty of paint for all the colours, and store the excess in 35mm film containers until required.

Fig 13.30 The black area of the head and the bill have been completed.

interface between the gray and the base coat, use a well-pointed brush and some of the reserved base coat.

Paint the primary feathers with mix B, which was used for the head, but leave the inner edges unpainted, showing the base coat. Darken the other wing feathers with a wash of mix D2, and then edge these with the base mix, mix A. Paint the quills of the primaries with mix A and a little flow medium, using a fine liner brush, and give them a very thin wash of mix B. Paint the other wing quills with mix B and a little flow medium, and when this is done, give all the quills a couple of coats of matt medium.

Repaint the underside of the wings with mix A, before applying a wash of mix D. Darken the outer edge of the feather with mix D2, and then paint the quill with mix A.

Treat the tail feathers like the underside of the wing, painting with mix A before applying a wash of mix D, and then darkening the outer edges with mix D2. As the upper surface is blacker than the lower surface, give it an additional wash of mix B. Paint the quills with mix A, and to finish, give them several coats of matt medium.

a fine lining brush. To finish the bill, give it several coats of matt medium on the outside, but only one coat on the inside.

The back area, painted with mix D, can be either wet blended onto the base coat, or airbrushed. (*See* Techniques in Chapter 10, on pages 76–79.) Create darker shadow areas to highlight the shape of the feathers, using the same mix darkened with just a little more black (mix D2). To tidy up the

Fig 13.31 Gray is added to the back and sides, and some underpainting done with a darker shade, using an airbrush, to add depth.

All that remains to do now is to highlight the feathers on the rump area with mix D, and to darken the lower chest and around the base with the same mix, blended to clean water on the base colour. (*See* Blending in Chapter 10, on page 77).

FINISHING AND ASSEMBLY

Remove the temporary base with one smart tap from a hammer, and try the whole composition together. To assemble the carving, screw the bird to its sub-base, and fix the whole assembly with a screw through the base; I glued it together later, when I was finally satisfied with the painting.

Fig 13.32 The primaries are painted dark gray and the hard-edged wing feathers have their details added.

Fig 13.33 Only the underside of the wings and the tail remain unpainted.

Fig 13.34 The underside of the primaries are painted.

Fig 13.35 Two
views of the finished
carving.

CHAPTER 14
ADDITIONAL PATTERNS

With the exception of the osprey and tern, all the patterns in this book are for birds of the woodland, stream and garden found in the Craven area of the Yorkshire Dales, where I live. At different times of the year the 'regulars' are supplemented by other species, and I can then study waders, raptors and other migrants at close quarters. I rarely venture out for a walk with Albert, my dog, without picking up my pocket binoculars. I am fortunate to have a large variety of species on my doorstep and my cottage forms a natural hide, situated as it is, next to a stream and wooded bank which provides a natural wildlife corridor.

The birds that I am inspired to draw and carve are generally the ones that I see regularly, or like the tern, that make a big impression on me when I encounter them. I am not a 'twitcher' and wouldn't even be classed a serious bird-watcher, but as a carver I take particular note of the species that interest me at the time and try to incorporate the essence of what I see into my drawings and carvings.

Drawings are only a starting point, and the draughtsman can only do some of the preparatory work for you; don't expect to create a good carving from a drawing alone, without studying the bird in depth first, and at least collecting a few photographs. You may have to travel to observe the bird you want, but you cannot beat having real visual experience of the bird when you come to assess your carving.

An early pair of gadwall (*Anas strepera*).

GREAT SPOTTED WOODPECKER

My favourite woodland bird, I took the great spotted woodpecker (*Dendrocopos major*) as my logo when I first started bird carving because they come and feed from the peanuts and suet that hang outside my studio window, just a couple of feet from me. The great spotted woodpecker is similar in size and Jizz to the North American red headed woodpecker. It is the most wide-spread of the British woodpeckers and is a regular visitor to bird tables, in areas where there are sufficient trees. Unlike the green woodpecker, they rarely feed on the ground, but are usually seen attacking rotten trees in search of grubs and insects. They call to each other by drumming on a resonant branch — one of mine discovered that an empty nestbox worked as a perfect amplifier and all but destroyed it in the process!

APPLYING THE COLOURS

Apply an undercoat of white acrylic gesso, then build up the black markings on the head, bill and wings with coats of mix A, using mix A2 for the final coat on the crown. Build up the colour on the cape, back and upper tail coverts and the long

centre tail feathers with mix B. Use straight Carbon Black, followed by matt medium, on the quills and bill. For the claws use mix B, and use a wash of mix B on the legs. Build up the tail markings with thin washes of mix C, and then tone down the white on the tail with a single thin wash. Apply mix D for the red undertail. Tone down the remaining white areas with a very thin wash of Raw Umber (Liquitex), leaving the cheek markings almost straight white; the breast and belly can be much darker. (A thin wash of mix C could be used to tone down the white underside instead of Raw Umber.)

COLOUR MIXES

MIX A	**MIX A2**	**MIX B**	**MIX C**	**MIX D**
Gray head markings, bill and wings	Green tint on crown	Black cape, back and upper tail coverts, and long, centre tail feathers	Brown tail markings	Red undertail
1 part Ultramarine (Rowney Cryla) to 1 part Burnt Sienna	Mix A plus a little Hooker's Green (Rowney Cryla)	1 part Ultramarine (Rowney Cryla) to 1 part Burnt Sienna to 1 part Carbon Black	1 part Burnt Umber to 1 part Carbon Black	Cadmium Red (Rowney Cryla) plus a little Deep Purple (Rowney Cryla)

Scale: Full size

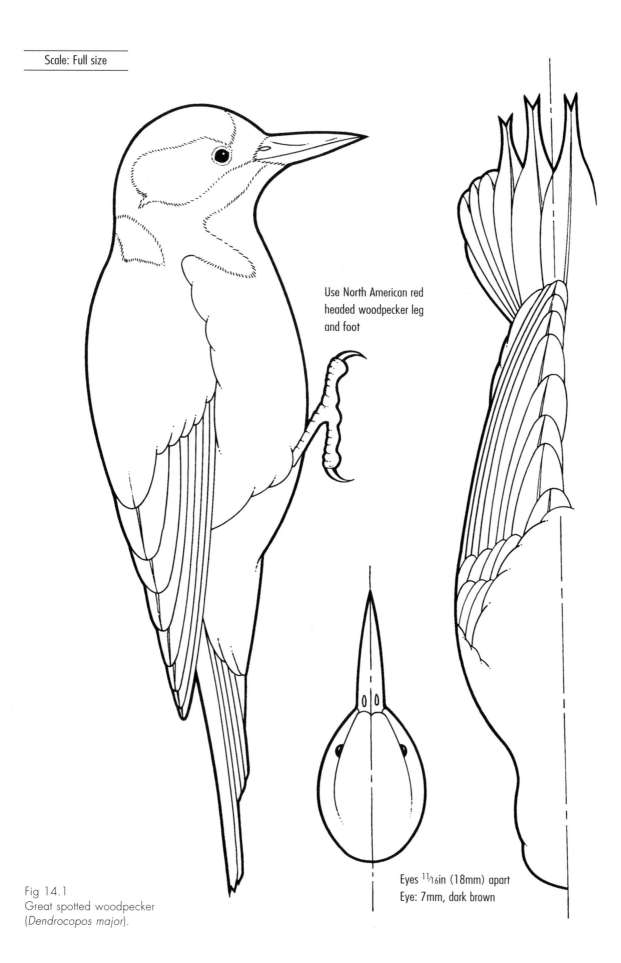

Use North American red
headed woodpecker leg
and foot

Eyes $^{11}/_{16}$in (18mm) apart
Eye: 7mm, dark brown

Fig 14.1
Great spotted woodpecker
(*Dendrocopos major*).

ROBIN

Chosen as Britain's national bird in 1961, the robin (*Erithacus rubecula*) is also one of the symbols of Christmas, along with snowmen and Santa Claus, appearing on many cards and calendars. The British robin is totally unlike its American namesake, which is a large red-breasted bird similar to our blackbird. A common garden bird, they are very tame, and will closely follow the footsteps of gardeners, waiting for an insect or tasty worm to be turned up. They are also fiercely territorial; defending their patch against interlopers is the robin's whole life, and rival males will sing all day to proclaim their territorial rights. Sleek in summer and rotund in winter, the 'robin redbreast' is an immediately recognizable denizen of the British garden.

APPLYING THE COLOURS

After applying the undercoat, build up the breast colours with mixes B and C. The colour here varies from a yellowish orange to a reddish brown. Darken the flanks with washes of Raw Umber or mix D. Build up the colour on the back and wings with coats of mix D, and the upper tail feathers with coats of mix E. For the lower tail feathers add a little gesso to mix E. To build up the dark brown of the quills, use mix E with a little Carbon Black added, and then apply several coats of matt medium. Edge the wing tips with the yellowish breast colour, mix B. Use a wash of mix E to darken the crown, and to build up the colour on the legs – don't get them too dark. For the claws apply coats of mix E, followed by coats of matt medium. Build up the colour of the bill, which is paler at the base and sides, with washes of mix E, then several coats of matt medium.

COLOUR MIXES

MIX A	**MIXES B AND C**	**MIX D**	**MIX E**
Gesso undercoat	Orange tones on breast	Green brown on back and wings	Brown on upper tail feathers
10 parts white acrylic gesso to 1 part Raw Umber	1 part Raw Sienna to 1 part Yellow Oxide, adding Norwegian Orange to give the desired shade	8 parts Raw Umber to 1 part Pine Green	5 parts Raw Umber to 1 part Burnt Umber plus a hint of white acrylic gesso

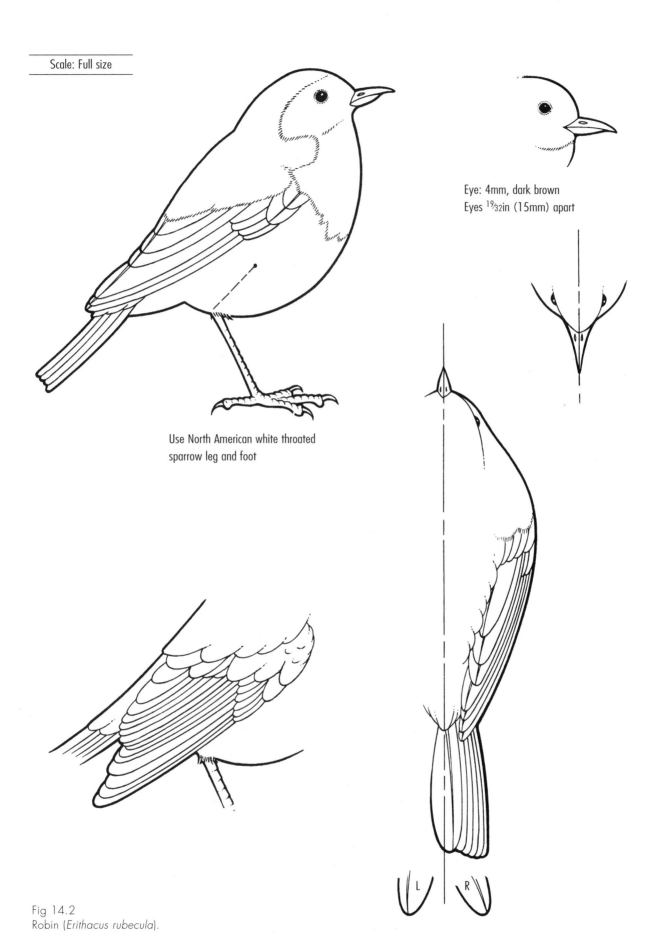

Scale: Full size

Eye: 4mm, dark brown
Eyes $^{19}/_{32}$in (15mm) apart

Use North American white throated
sparrow leg and foot

L   R

Fig 14.2
Robin (*Erithacus rubecula*).

BARN SWALLOW

It was recently decided that the bird we have always called a swallow (*Hirundo rustica*) is now to be called a barn swallow, to bring its name in line with its American relations! When not on the wing, overhead wires are their favourite resting places, and their mud nests, under the eaves of houses and in outbuildings, are a familiar sight. Barn swallows are one of the early signs of summer; the first birds arrive in late spring and sit twittering on the telephone lines, indicating that summer is on its way. As spring turns into summer the numbers swell, and they practise graceful aerobatic displays in search of flying insects. All too soon they start to gather in large chattering flocks, then overnight are gone, and with them goes the summer. Their graceful shapes and subtle colours make them an interesting subject to carve.

APPLYING THE COLOURS

Once the undercoat has dried, use thin washes of mix B to build up colour on the undersides of the wings and tail. Use mix B for the legs and claws as well, using washes for the legs, and the straight mix for the claws. Apply coats of mix C to the cape, crown and bill, and use mix C2 for the final washes on the cape and crown. Build up the red on the chin with mix D.

COLOUR MIXES

MIX A	MIX B	MIX C	MIX C2	MIX D
Gesso undercoat	Brown on wings, tail and chest	Blue on cape, crown of head and bill	Washes on cape and crown of head	Red on chin
White acrylic gesso plus a minute amount of 2 parts Raw Umber (Liquitex) to 1 part Burnt Sienna	1 part Burnt Umber to 1 part Ultramarine (Rowney Cryla)	3 parts Ultramarine (Rowney Cryla) to 1 part Burnt Umber	Mix C plus a little blue pearlescent powder	2 parts Burnt Sienna to 1 part Napthol Red Light

Scale: 70% (enlarge by 141% for full size)

Eye: 4mm, black ball/dark brown
Eyes $^{15}/_{32}$in (12mm) apart

Use North American
goldfinch leg and foot

Remember: Open wings are not
flat like a plank; they have an
aerofoil section and all surfaces are
curved in flight

Fig 14.3
Barn swallow (*Hirundo rustica*).

BLUE TIT

The most common member of the tit family, the blue tit (*Parus caeruleus*) is a brave, agile and intelligent acrobat, with a presence beyond its physical size. It provides hours of entertainment for owners of nestboxes and feeders throughout Europe. It is similar to, but slightly smaller than the North American chickadee. Blue tits are really a woodland bird, but have adapted well to life in parks, and especially in gardens. In winter, the wooded bank behind my studio is host to large, mixed feeding parties consisting mainly of blue tits, but also including great, coal and long-tailed tits, nuthatches, tree-creepers, goldcrests and wrens. Blue tits are the boldest defenders of a place on the peanut feeder, often repelling larger species. They are probably the easiest species to attract to gardens with a nesting box, hence my design for one popping out of the entrance hole of a box, which makes a good wall plaque or bookend with the sort of 'cute factor' appeal that would make it a popular present.

APPLYING THE COLOURS

After applying the undercoat, apply coats of mix B to build up the black markings on the face and chin. Use mix B2 for the bill, keeping it paler at the sides. For the bluish head, upper tail and wings apply coats of mix C, for the back mix D, and for the belly mix E. Use only thin washes of mix F for the pale gray of the wings and the underside of the tail, and apply coats of mix G to build up the colour of the legs and claws, leaving the claws a lighter shade.

COLOUR MIXES

MIX A
Gesso undercoat

White acrylic gesso plus a little Payne's Gray

MIX B
Black face markings and chin

1 part Burnt Sienna to 2 parts Ultramarine (Rowney Cryla)

MIX B2
Black markings on bill

Mix B plus a little Burnt Sienna

MIX C
Blue on head, upper tail and wings

1 part Burnt Sienna to 3 parts Ultramarine (Rowney Cryla)

MIX D
Green on back

3 parts Yellow Light to 1 part Ultramarine (Rowney Cryla)

MIX E
Yellow on belly

1 part mix D to 3 parts Yellow Light

MIX F
Gray on underside of tail and wings

1 part Raw Umber to 1 part Carbon Black

MIX G
Dark gray on legs and claws

1 part Burnt Umber to 1 part Carbon Black

Scale: Full size

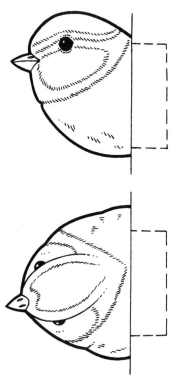

Eye: 4mm, black ball
Eyes $^{13}/_{32}$in (11)mm apart

Nest box version: turn or carve a spigot on a rectangular blank to fit the nest box hole before sawing the profiles

Use North American house wren leg and foot

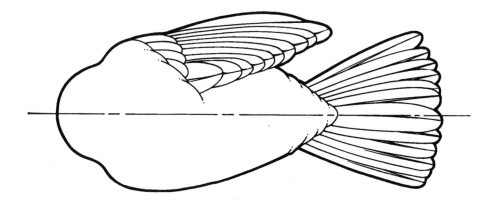

Fig 14.4
Blue tit (*Parus caeruleus*).

KINGFISHER

Unless you are lucky enough to watch one perched, a brilliant flash of electric blue and orange/chestnut flying along a stream or river is all you will see of Britain's most exotically plumaged bird. When the river near me is in flood, I am sometimes lucky enough to spot a kingfisher (*Alcedo atthis*) perched on a branch, searching for small trout in the stream behind my house. Although it is a relatively easy bird to carve and mount, the painting is more than somewhat challenging. It is extremely difficult to do justice to the vibrant colours of its plumage, and much trial and error will be needed to create anything better than a pale imitation of the real bird. I have only seen one carved kingfisher with a really successful paint job, so this is a real challenge for your painting skills.

APPLYING THE COLOURS

Apply an undercoat of white acrylic gesso, and then apply coats of mixes A1 and A2 to build up the orange colours on the breast, the eye stripe and the edges of the white face markings. The green on the crown and cape is built up with coats of mix B, and the feather markings painted over this, first with white gesso, and then with mix C. Use mix C for the upper tail coverts and back as well, making sure that it is used over the white gesso. For the blue of the tail feathers use mix D, and mix D2 for the darker feather shafts. Mix E will give the brown for the primary feathers and the underside of the tail. Use mix F for the bill, blending a little of the chestnut breast colour (mix A) near the base, then applying several coats of matt medium. For the orange red legs use mix A2 blended with a little more Napthol Red Light, and use mix E for the brownish claws.

COLOUR MIXES

MIX A1

Rust on the breast, eye stripe and edges of the white face markings

2 parts Burnt Sienna to 2 parts Cadmium Orange (Rowney Cryla) to 1 part Yellow Oxide

MIX A2

Colour variation for a more orange rust

1 part Cadmium Orange (Rowney Cryla) to 1 part Raw Umber to 1 part Napthol Red Light

MIX B

Green on crown and cape

1 part Pine Green to 1 part Ultramarine (Rowney Cryla)

MIX C

Turquoise on upper tail coverts and back

1 part Monestial Green (Rowney Cryla) to 1 part Monestial Blue (Rowney Cryla) to 1 part Iridescent Silver (Spectracryl) (white pearlescent powder can be used instead of Iridescent Silver)

MIX D

Blue on upperside of tail feathers

2 parts Payne's Gray to 1 part Ultramarine (Rowney Cryla)

MIX D2

Blue-black on feather shafts

Mix D plus a little Carbon Black

MIX E

Brown on primary feathers and underside of tail

2 parts Carbon Black to 2 parts Raw Umber to 1 part Burnt Sienna

MIX F

Dark gray on bill

1 part Ultramarine (Rowney Cryla) to 1 part Burnt Sienna

Scale: Full size

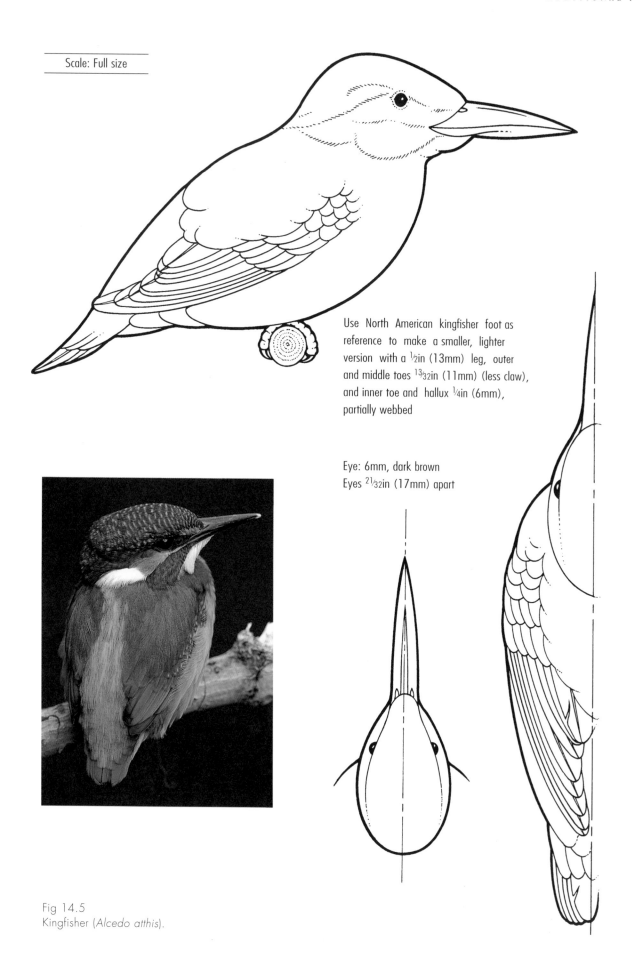

Use North American kingfisher foot as reference to make a smaller, lighter version with a ¹⁄₂in (13mm) leg, outer and middle toes ¹³⁄₃₂in (11mm) (less claw), and inner toe and hallux ¹⁄₄in (6mm), partially webbed

Eye: 6mm, dark brown
Eyes ²¹⁄₃₂in (17mm) apart

Fig 14.5
Kingfisher (*Alcedo atthis*).

GOLDFINCH

Even in its breeding plumage, the Eurasian goldfinch (*Carduelis carduelis*) is not as colourful as its American namesake, but it is my favourite amongst the birds to be found in the fields near my home. The protection of these attractive little birds was one of the first conservation projects undertaken by the RSPB (Royal Society for the Protection of Birds). Their existence in the wild was threatened by their popularity as caged songbirds in the nineteenth century, in the middle of which, it was reported that as many as 132,000 birds a year were being caught in just one area – near Worthing in East Sussex. Changes in agricultural practice also reduced the abundance of thistles and weeds, whose seeds form a major part of the goldfinch's diet, but despite this, they have found new feeding areas created by roads and industry and have survived to delight us today. Goldfinches are tree nesting and like relatively open spaces. Their red face and bright yellow wing bars make them easily recognizable. Small flocks, called charms, are often to be seen in late summer and autumn, feeding on the seed heads of thistles, grasses and other plants.

APPLYING THE COLOURS

Apply the gesso undercoat, which is a little off-white, and then build up the browns on the chest and back with mix A. The back is darker, so will need more coats. For the pale brown of the bill use a thin wash of mix A and blend in Burnt Umber on the tip. Use mix C for the red cheek markings and Mix D for the yellow wing markings. Build up the black markings on the head, wings and upper tail with washes of mix E, adding a very small amount of blue pearlescent powder to the final wash on the wings.

COLOUR MIXES

MIX A	MIX B	MIX C	MIX D	MIX E
Gesso undercoat	Brown on chest and back	Red cheek marks	Yellow wing marking	Black markings on head, wings and upper tail
10 parts white acrylic gesso to 1 part Raw Umber (Liquitex)	2 parts Raw Umber (Liquitex) to 2 parts Raw Sienna	4 parts Napthol Red Light to 2 parts Iridescent Silver* (Spectracryl) to 1 part Deep Violet (Rowney Cryla)	Azo Yellow Medium (Windsor and Newton) plus a small amount of Raw Umber (Liquitex)	2 parts Ultramarine (Rowney Cryla) to 1 part Carbon Black

*white pearlescent powder can be used instead of Iridescent Silver

Scale: Full size

Eye: 4mm, black ball
Eyes $^{13}/_{32}$in (11mm)
apart

Use North American house
wren leg and foot

Fig 14.6
Goldfinch (*Carduelis carduelis*).

OSPREY

Most of my favourite birds are ones that frequent the area where I live or the places I regularly visit. However, in the case of birds of prey, my admiration extends beyond the peregrines, sparrowhawks and kestrels which I regularly see to include the osprey (*Pandion haliateus*). Missing from Britain for 50 years, the first ospreys returned to Loch Garten to breed when I was a schoolboy, and to my shame I still haven't joined the thousands who visit their Speyside, RSPB nesting sight. They are found throughout the northern hemisphere, and breed near both fresh and salt water. I have seen non-breeding birds at inland sites many times over the years, and they remain one of my favourite birds of prey. Their diet consists almost entirely of fish, their talons are unusual in that they are round in section, and their feet have very rough pads – an adaptation which helps them to catch and keep hold of the slippery customers. A full-sized bird is somewhat of a mammoth task to carve, so it is an ideal candidate for carving in miniature, and the drawing was prepared with this in mind, rather than a full-sized bird. The osprey's habit of using isolated, dead trees for nesting and feeding sights makes this an obvious way to display the carving, giving it height from the display surface and making an impressive bird, even at this small scale.

APPLYING THE COLOURS

Once the undercoat has been applied, build up the eye stripe and the dark markings on the head with mix B. Mix B can also be used on the body, but it is often more brownish, so mix C may be more appropriate. The feather edges are lighter and vary in tone: try either of the mix D's. Use washes of mix E for the fleshy part at the base of the bill, and mix F for the rest of the bill. For the legs apply a thin wash of mix B, and for the talons, mix F.

COLOUR MIXES

MIX A
Gesso undercoat

White acrylic gesso plus a hint of Payne's Gray

MIX B
Dark eye stripe and head markings

2½ parts Ultramarine (Rowney Cryla) to 2 parts Burnt Umber

MIX C
Dark brown on body

1 part Ultramarine (Rowney Cryla) to 2 parts Burnt Umber

MIX D1
Lighter brown on feather edges

4 parts Raw Sienna to 1 part Mix B2

MIX D2
Colour variation for lighter brown on feather edges

1 part Mix A to 1 part Mix B2

MIX E
Gray on base of bill

White acrylic gesso plus a small amount 4 parts Payne's Gray to 1 part Carbon Black

MIX F
Dark gray on bill

1 part Ultramarine (Rowney Cryla) to 1 part Carbon Black

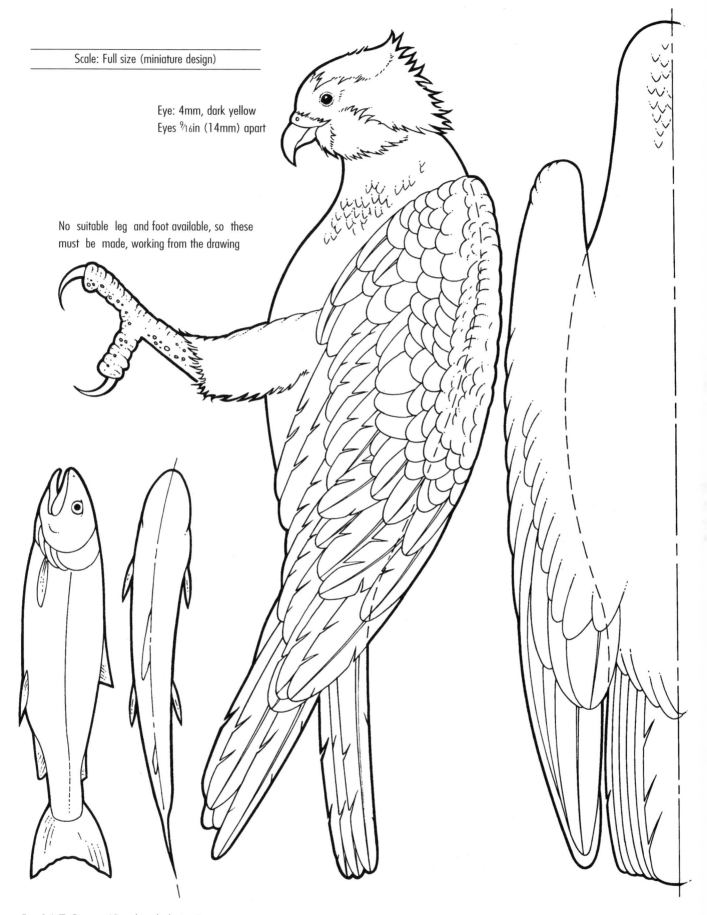

Scale: Full size (miniature design)

Eye: 4mm, dark yellow
Eyes $^9/_{16}$in (14mm) apart

No suitable leg and foot available, so these
must be made, working from the drawing

Fig 14.7 Osprey (*Pandion haliateus*).

RECOMMENDED READING

This is not an exhaustive list, but rather, a personal selection of what I consider the best of my now extensive (and expensive) bookshelf. These are the titles I would buy again if my bookshelf caught fire!

BOOKS

BADGER C AND SPRANKLE D, *Painting Waterfowl with J D Sprankle,* (ISBN 0 8117 1884 0), Stackpole Books, Harrisburg, Pennsylvania, USA, 1991

Superbly detailed painting instruction for ducks, but the techniques are equally applicable to all birds.

BROWN R, FERGUSON J, LAWRENCE M, LEES D, *Tracks and Signs of Birds of Britain and Europe: An Identification Guide,* (ISBN 0 7136 3523 1), Christopher Helm, London, UK, 1992

This book is excellent for details of feathers, including feather shape and count.

BURK B, *Game Bird Carving,* 3rd ed, (ISBN 0 8329 0439 2), New Win Publishing, Hampton, New Jersey, USA, 1988

Now in its third edition, this book is considered by many to be *the* encyclopaedia of bird carving.

DAISEY R L, *Shorebird Carving,* (ISBN 0 88740 219 4), Schiffer Publishing, Chester, Pennsylvania, USA, 1990

A beautifully produced and highly detailed book. The author has also written other bird carving books, although these are not as relevant to European carvers.

GINN H B AND MELVILLE D S, *Moult in Birds,* (ISBN 0 903793 02 4), British Trust for Ornithology, Tring, Hertfordshire, UK, 1983

If you have ever wondered just how many feathers that tail or wing should have, this is the ideal, affordable reference book. (Intended mainly for bird ringers.) If you can't find the information on a particular bird in this book, the following three identification guides are also available through the British Trust for Ornithology, Tring, Hertfordshire, UK: *Guide to Identification and Aging of Holarctic Waders* (Prater, Marchant and Vuorinen); *Identification Guide of European Passerines* (Svensson, L); *Identification Guide of European Non-Passerines* (Baker, K).

METCALF, C, Taxidermy; A Complete Manual, (ISBN 0 7156 1565 3), Duckworth, London, 1981

This book will tell you how to make a study skin from the latest feline offering, and it has a very good section on eye sizes and colours for a wide variety of birds – very useful!

MUEHLMATT E, *Songbird Carving,* (ISBN 0 8117 1817 4), Stackpole Books, Harrisburg, Pennsylvania, USA, 1987

This contains American species, but most can be adapted to a similar European one.

SCHOLTZ F, *Birds of Prey,* (ISBN 0 8117 0242 1), Stackpole Books, Harrisburg, Pennsylvania, USA, 1993

The most wonderful reference photographs of diurnal raptors!

SCHROEDER R, *Wildfowl Carving,* (ISBN 1 800 732 3669), Stackpole Books, Harrisburg, Pennsylvania, USA, 1992

Containing the work of some of the top American bird carvers, this book will either inspire you or make you put away your tools for life!

SCHROEDER R AND SPRANKLE J D, *Waterfowl Carving with J D Sprankle,* (ISBN 0 8117 1856 5), Stackpole Books, Harrisburg, Pennsylvania, USA, 1985

Follow this book to radically improve your duck carving!

The work of bird artists is often informative and stimulating when looking for good ideas for carvings. I have collected books on the work of many artists, and can highly recommend the following books, and any others including their work.

BROCKIE K, *One Man's Island*, (ISBN 0 460 12549 4), J M Dent & Sons Ltd, London, UK, 1984

TUNNICLIFFE, C F, *A Sketchbook of Birds* (introduction by Ian Nial) , (ISBN 0 575 02640 5), Victor Gollancz Ltd, London, UK, 1979

A range of useful and cheap reference books on individual species, including some photographs, are published in the Shire Natural History series from: Shire Publications Ltd, Princes Risborough, Buckinghamshire, UK

MAGAZINES

Various magazines and journals covering birds and woodcarving are available. I am a regular purchaser of the following:

UNITED KINGDOM

Birdwatch, Solo Publishing Ltd, London, UK

Birdwatching, EMAP Pursuit Publishing, Bretton, Peterborough, UK

These first two magazines are a must for good reference photographs.

Woodcarving, GMC Publications, Lewes, East Sussex, UK

Birdcarving is frequently included in *Woodcarving*.

UNITED STATES

Chip Chats, National Wood Carvers Association, Cincinnati, Oklahoma, USA (Members journal, only available by subscription)

Including quite a lot of birdcarvings, this one comes at a bargain price! *Chip Chats* is full of ideas and inspiration for woodcarving.

Wildfowl Carving & Collecting, Stackpole, Harrisburg, Pennsylvania, USA

Rather expensive for a magazine, *Wildfowl Carving & Collecting* is, nevertheless, of very high quality, and one I really look forward to receiving.

VIDEOS

BBC RSPB FILM AND VIDEO UNIT, AND BIRD GUIDES produce video footage of various European species. Some are like a field guide, covering many birds, sometimes as briefly as 15 seconds of film, while others, including much of the BBC RSPB output, have a full programme devoted to one species.

BBC RSPB, *Video Guide to Garden Birds*

BBC RSPB, *Osprey*

BBC RSPB, *Kingfisher: Secret Splendour of the Brooks/The Short-Eared Owl*

BBC RSPB, *Round Robin/Tit mice*

BIRD GUIDES, *Video Guide to British Birds* (a five volume work; can be bought in single volumes)

BIRD GUIDES, *CD Rom Guide to British Birds* (includes video clips)

These videos are available from:

Video Plus Direct
19-24 Manasty Rd
Orton, Southgate
Peterborough PE2 6UP

RSPB Film and Video Unit
The Lodge
Sandy
Bedfordshire SG19 2DL

Bird Guides Ltd
PO Box 471
Sheffield S6 2YT

Carving Clubs and Associations

British Decoy Wildfowl Carvers Association
Membership Secretary, 6 Pendred Rd, Reading, Berkshire RG2 8QL, UK

Members receive regular newsletters, and there is an annual show and competition. There are various local groups around the UK, including a Northwestern one organized by the author.

British Woodcarvers Association
Secretary, John Sullivan, 25 Summerfield Drive, Porthcawl CF36 3PB, UK

Much more general in scope, nonetheless many members carve birds, particularly natural finished ones. There are various regional groups, organized shows and a regular newsletter.

National Wood Carvers Association
PO Box 43218, Cincinnati, Oklahoma, 45243-0218, USA

This association produces the superb bi-monthly magazine *Chip Chats*. It's full of hints and tips, photographs of all types and standards of woodcarving, and information on exhibitions and other carving clubs in the USA. It really is a good woodcarving magazine, without all the advertisements, and all for $14 per year!

METRIC CONVERSION TABLE

INCHES TO MILLIMETRES AND CENTIMETRES

mm = millimetres   cm = centimetres

INCHES	MM	CM	INCHES	CM	INCHES	CM
⅛	3	0.3	9	22.9	30	76.2
¼	6	0.6	10	25.4	31	78.7
⅜	10	1.0	11	27.9	32	81.3
½	13	1.3	12	30.5	33	83.8
⅝	16	1.6	13	33.0	34	86.4
¾	19	1.9	14	35.6	35	88.9
⅞	22	2.2	15	38.1	36	91.4
1	25	2.5	16	40.6	37	94.0
1¼	32	3.2	17	43.2	38	96.5
1½	38	3.8	18	45.7	39	99.1
1¾	44	4.4	19	48.3	40	101.6
2	51	5.1	20	50.8	41	104.1
2½	64	6.4	21	53.3	42	106.7
3	76	7.6	22	55.9	43	109.2
3½	89	8.9	23	58.4	44	111.8
4	102	10.2	24	61.0	45	114.3
4½	114	11.4	25	63.5	46	116.8
5	127	12.7	26	66.0	47	119.4
6	152	15.2	27	68.6	48	121.9
7	178	17.8	28	71.1	49	124.5
8	203	20.3	29	73.7	50	127.0

INDEX

ABOUT THE AUTHOR

David Tippey's interests in woodworking and metalwork were natural developments from his interest in model making, which began when he was a teenager. On finishing school he went on to study photography at Kitson College in Leeds, before joining industry. He became the technical director of a Harrogate electronics company, manufacturing printed circuits, until in 1984 he changed career to become landlord of a pub in the Yorkshire Dales.

His spare time interests have always been practical, spanning a wide range of projects, from model boats, aeroplanes and amateur radio as a teenager, to antique restoration, model engineering and silverwork, but these all took a back seat after a magazine article on American decoys prompted the purchase of a book on decoy carving, and his first carvings emerged. Since the opportunity to carve full time arose in 1988, the scope and style of his carving has increased, moving away from just the decoy duck to a much wider avian theme.

For a complete change from the highly detailed style covered in this book, David also carves stylized, simply painted, birds which draw their inspiration from the flowing, graceful shapes of their subjects, and occasionally, an engagingly simple, tactile, natural finish wooden bird, revealing the beauty of the wood from which it is fashioned.

His work has found its way into collections in Britain, Europe and North America, and has been featured in various magazines and on television. He regularly writes articles and reviews for woodworking magazines, and is also active in teaching woodcarving, running courses at local colleges, and individual birdcarving courses at his own studio.

David is the founder of the Northwestern Group of the British Decoy Wildfowl Carvers Association, so almost all of his time is dedicated to carving in some form or other. The great spotted woodpecker has become his logo.

TITLES AVAILABLE
FROM GUILD OF MASTER CRAFTSMAN PUBLICATIONS

BOOKS

Carving Birds and Beasts . . . . GMC Publications
Faceplate Turning . . . . GMC Publications
Practical Tips for Turners and Carvers . . . . GMC Publications
Practical Tips for Woodturners . . . . GMC Publications
Spindle Turning . . . . GMC Publications
Useful Woodturning Projects . . . . GMC Publications
Woodturning Techniques . . . . GMC Publications
Woodworkers' Career and Educational Source Book . . . . GMC Publications
Woodworking Plans and Projects . . . . GMC Publications
40 More Woodworking Plans and Projects . . . . GMC Publications
Green Woodwork . . . . Mike Abbott
Easy to Make Dolls' House Accessories . . . . Andrea Barham
Making Little Boxes from Wood . . . . John Bennett
Woodturning Masterclass . . . . Tony Boase
Furniture Restoration and Repair for Beginners . . . . Kevin Jan Bonner
Woodturning Jewellery . . . . Hilary Bowen
The Incredible Router . . . . Jeremy Broun
Electric Woodwork . . . . Jeremy Broun
Woodcarving: A Complete Course . . . . Ron Butterfield
Making Fine Furniture: Projects . . . . Tom Darby
Restoring Rocking Horses . . . . Clive Green & Anthony Dew
Make Your Own Dolls' House Furniture . . . . Maurice Harper
Embroidery Tips and Hints . . . . Harold Hayes
Seat Weaving . . . . Ricky Holdstock
Multi-centre Woodturning . . . . Ray Hopper
Complete Woodfinishing . . . . Ian Hosker
Woodfinishing Handbook . . . . Ian Hosker
Woodturning: A Source Book of Shapes . . . . John Hunnex
Illustrated Woodturning Techniques . . . . John Hunnex
Making Shaker Furniture . . . . Barry Jackson
Upholstery: A Complete Course . . . . David James
Upholstery Techniques and Projects . . . . David James
The Upholsterer's Pocket Reference Book . . . . David James
Designing and Making Wooden Toys . . . . Terry Kelly
Making Dolls' House Furniture . . . . Patricia King
Making Victorian Dolls' House Furniture . . . . Patricia King
Making and Modifying Woodworking Tools . . . . Jim Kingshott
The Workshop . . . . Jim Kingshott
Sharpening: The Complete Guide . . . . Jim Kingshott
Sharpening Pocket Reference Book . . . . Jim Kingshott
Turning Wooden Toys . . . . Terry Lawrence
Making Board, Peg and Dice Games . . . . Jeff & Jennie Loader
Making Wooden Toys and Games . . . . Jeff & Jennie Loader
Bert Marsh: Woodturner . . . . Bert Marsh
The Complete Dolls' House Book . . . . Jean Nisbett
The Secrets of the Dolls' House Makers . . . . Jean Nisbett
Wildfowl Carving, Volume 1 . . . . Jim Pearce

VIDEOS

GMC Publications regularly produces new books and videos on a wide range of woodworking and craft subjects, and an increasing number of specialist magazines, all available on subscription:

MAGAZINES

Woodturning   Woodcarving   Businessmatters

All these publications are available through bookshops and newsagents, or may be ordered by post from the publishers at Castle Place, 166 High Street, Lewes, East Sussex BN7 1XU
Telephone (01273) 477374, Fax (01273) 478606

Credit card orders are accepted

PLEASE WRITE OR PHONE FOR A FREE CATALOGUE